# THE
# CREATIVE
# NURSERY

# THE
# CREATIVE
# NURSERY

# LINDA BARKER

a Salamander book

**Published by Salamander Books Limited**
**LONDON**

A SALAMANDER BOOK

Published by Salamander Books Ltd
129-137 York Way
London N7 9LG
United Kingdom

© Salamander Books Ltd, 1995

Distributed by Random House Value Publishing, Inc.
40 Engelhard Avenue
Avenel
New Jersey 07001

A CIP catalog record for this book is available from the Library of Congress

1 3 5 7 9 8 6 4 2

ISBN 0-517-12155-7

All correspondence concerning the content of this volume
should be addressed to Salamander Books Ltd.

**Commissioning Editor:** Lisa Dyer
**Editor:** Ian Penberthy
**Photographer:** Lizzie Orme
**Stylist:** Linda Barker
**Project Maker:** Sally Barker
**Artwork:** Malcolm Porter
**Design:** Rachel Griffin & Ian Penberthy
**Color Separation:** Pixel Tech Prepress PTE Ltd

Printed in Spain

# CONTENTS

# INTRODUCTION

*T*he nursery is one of the most rewarding rooms to decorate, quite unlike the laborious chores of having to paint the kitchen or wallpaper the living room. Planning a nursery is an exciting project; it's fun and a great test of your imagination. Packed with wonderful projects that anyone can make, this fascinating book is just as much fun to use and as exciting to comb for ideas that will make the nursery a thrilling place for your children.

**Below:** *Some of the many materials needed to make the 'soft' projects in this book. They include offcuts of fabric, fabric glue, coloured paper, pencils, cottons, beads, dressmaker's pins, drawing pins and scissors.*

The projects outlined in this book are designed to inspire your creativity. Beautifully-photographed step-by-step instructions will help to guide you through the individual projects, while lots of helpful hints have been included to make the different tasks as simple as possible.

Most of the materials and tools needed to create the projects in this book can be divided into two specific categories: 'soft' and 'hard'. Those

for the 'soft' projects include threads and pins, needles and scissors, felt, ribbon, fabric and toy stuffing, as well as paints, glues, clear acetate and tissue paper. The remaining projects are constructed from solid materials, like hardboard, plywood and wire, as in 'The Cow Jumped Over the Moon Lightshade' and the 'Cat Mirror'. These require materials such as wood and chicken wire, as well as tools like pliers, glass-paper and wire cutters.

## Scaling Up the Design

Each of the book's projects will guide you through all of the steps needed for construction, so you will be able to create some wonderful pieces quickly and with little fuss. Many projects feature scaled-down patterns of the design, which have been drawn onto a grid. The grid will help you draw the pattern to the final size you require and is quite simple to use. Each grid is marked with the scale: for example, 'One square represents 2.5cm (1in)'. Use this scale to draw your own full-size grid onto a sheet of paper using a pencil and a rule.

Once your grid is finished, you can transfer the drawing onto it from the page. To do this, you must choose a point on the pattern at which to start and find the corresponding square on your own grid. Determine where the pattern enters and leaves the square, mark these points, then join them, carefully following the shape of the pattern within the square.

Continue to carefully copy the pattern, square by square, and when the outline has been filled in, add the details within the pattern. Most of the designs in the book can be scaled up or down as necessary to suit your own requirements - all you need do is draw a grid either larger or smaller than the suggested size. Alternatively, you could even use the

enlarging and reducing facilities of a good photocopying machine.

## Using the Pattern

In some cases, you can simply use your paper pattern for creating the design, either by cutting the pattern into its individual pieces or by tracing through it with the aid of carbon paper. In others, however, it may be easier to transfer the pattern to cardboard to make templates, which can be traced around. Either draw out your grid directly onto the cardboard or glue the paper patterns to it, then cut out the shapes. One advantage of making cardboard templates is that they are durable, allowing them to be used time and again.

## Materials and Tools

Each nursery project includes a list of materials and tools that you will need, so you can be sure that everything is to hand before you begin. Most materials can be found in craft shops and hardware stores. Often, you may find them at home, while some of the projects even make use of materials that normally would be thrown away. For example, the very charismatic 'Decorative Aquarium' is made from an old cardboard box, and the tiny fish that sway around inside come from plastic bottles.

If you enjoy crafts or other practical hobbies, you may find that you already have most items required, but if you are an absolute beginner, you will need to spend a little money for things like poster paints, brushes, and an assortment of pencils and pens. Always buy good-quality paint brushes and paints: cheap brushes leave their hairs in a newly-painted surface, while budget paints offer poor coverage with lots of streaking. Moreover, good-quality materials will reflect in the end product, while good tools will repay their expense with a long, useful life.

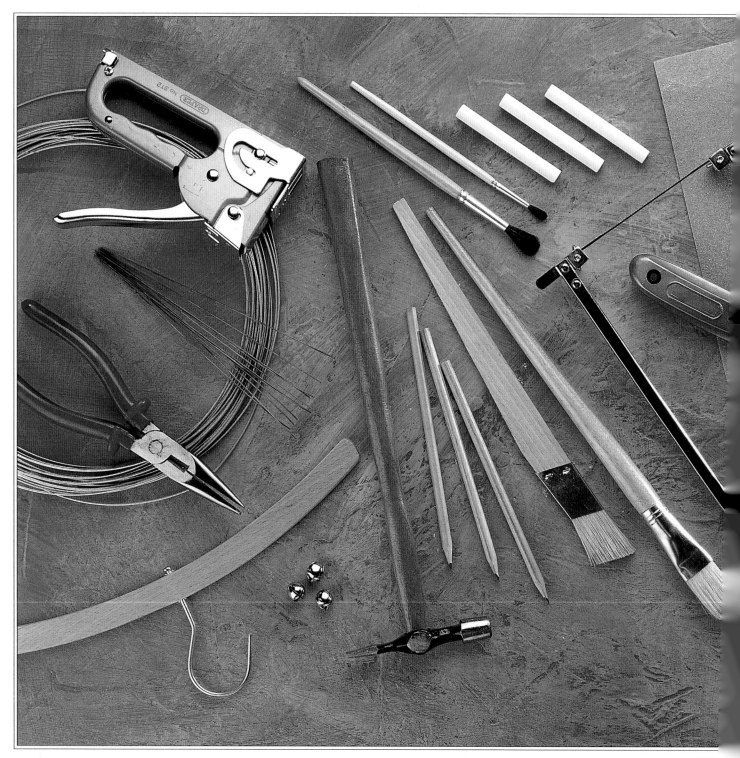

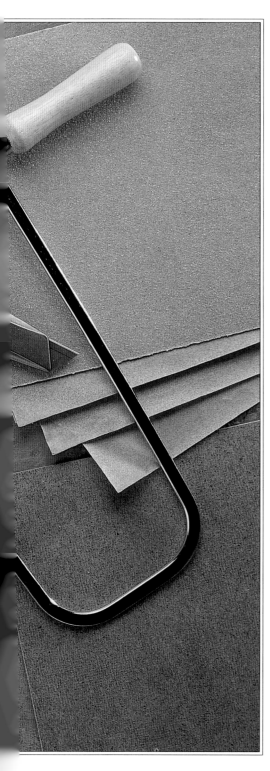

**Left:** *Some of the materials and tools you will need to complete the 'hard' designs in the book. These include hardboard, glass-paper, a fret saw, a hammer, wire cutters, florist's wire, pencils, paint brushes, a stapler, a craft knife and coat hangers.*

## Using a Fret Saw

*Some of the projects in this book need cutting out with a fret saw, which is an easy tool to use once you have made the first cut. If you need further encouragement, just look at the projects you will be able to make when you have mastered the technique.*

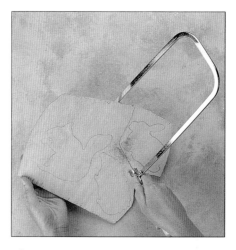

*1 To begin a fretwork project, you must first copy or scale-up the pattern onto a sheet of paper. Then trace or draw the outline onto your piece of hardboard or plywood. You can use a pencil for this, but a marker pen will make a much more legible and easily-followed mark.*

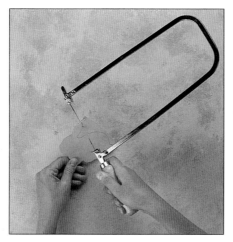

*2 Roughly cut the shape from the panel of wood, holding the fret saw as shown here. Use the blade with a slight up-and-down movement. At first, you may experience a jerky movement as the teeth pass through the wood, but with a little practice this should become much smoother.*

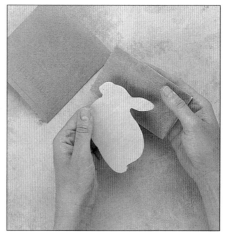

*3 Once the pattern has been roughly cut out, you can trim it to the final shape. Follow the outline carefully, using the same technique as before and keeping the blade moving all the time. Turn the wood to allow the blade to follow the curves of the pattern. Finally, smooth the cut edges with glass-paper.*

# POTATO PRINT WALL

*W*e've all probably experimented with potato printing at some time in our lives, most likely when we were very young, using lots of runny paint and usually producing a sludgy mess. The decoration on these walls is printed using exactly the same method, albeit a little more controlled. The stars and moons are cut from potatoes with a sharp craft knife, rather than an ordinary kitchen knife, to produce the fine detailing.

**You will need:**
Potatoes
Brown paper and tracing paper
Pencil or marker pen
Kitchen roll
Pins
Craft knife or cutting tool
Artist's brush and emulsion paint

It is really very simple to decorate your walls using potato prints; once the design is cut, you'll have the whole nursery finished in next to no time. Choose large baking potatoes rather than smaller new potatoes, otherwise you will experience difficulty in fitting the templates on the cut surface. Don't be tempted to reduce the scale of the motifs, thinking that smaller stars may look more attractive, as the shapes will lose some of the definition. Use emulsion colours for printing and brush the paint onto the surface of the potato, rather than dipping the potato into the paint; this will result in a much clearer pattern.

## Sharp Points

Trace around the shapes on page 12 and cut out the stars and the moons to make paper templates. Each of the shapes is cut into half of a potato. Fix the template to the cut surface of the potato with dressmaker's pins so that it is held securely while you cut around it. A sharp knife will produce the best results, as it is important to ensure that the motif has straight, clean sides and that the stars have sharp points with no rough, ragged edges.

Occasionally you may find that a print hasn't come out as well as it should. Don't press the potato back over the print in an attempt to fill in the missing detail; it is too easy to twist the potato slightly, making the whole print messy. Instead, fill in any gaps left by the bad print with the paint brush. Use the brush with a stippling motion, filling in the areas that haven't printed with a small amount of paint.

1 *Trace the templates from the page and transfer to brown paper. Alternatively, you may wish to hold the page up to a window, place your brown paper over the top and draw around the shapes in this way. Light shining through the paper enables you to see the shapes well enough to be able to draw around them. Cut the shapes from the paper.*

**Right:** *Using potato prints is an easy and effective means of brightening up your nursery's walls. It's also inexpensive and fun, allowing you to give free rein to your imagination and creative skills. Simply apply the prints directly to a painted surface, using emulsion paint.*

2 *Cut the potato in half and use kitchen roll to dry the cut face. Place the paper template on the surface, turning it until the shape fits neatly within the cut area. Hold the template securely with a few dressmaker's pins if necessary. Then use a craft knife or cutting tool to pare away the excess potato around the shape.*

If you prefer, you could mark the wall lightly before you begin, using a piece of chalk or a pencil to indicate the positions of the prints. However, it can be just as effective to build up the design using a casual arrangement of the various motifs.

**Right:** *Use these star and moon shapes full size, tracing them onto brown paper to make templates that can be pinned to the cut faces of the potatoes. Then trim around the shapes with a sharp knife to produce a raised pattern.*

**3** *Brush paint onto the surface of the cut potato, using a flat artist's brush for best results; a regular paint brush may overload the paint, resulting in a smudged pattern. Try to apply an even coat of paint so that there are no dense or light patches to spoil the effect. Practise printing on scrap paper first.*

**4** *Once you are ready to start printing, press the potato firmly onto the wall. Apply light pressure around the outside of the potato, then pull it away to reveal the print underneath. Progress around the room using one motif, then move on to the other shapes, filling gaps until the wall is finished.*

# BABY QUILT

*Making a soft quilt need not be a daunting prospect: it's really much easier than you might think. This beautiful baby's quilt has been made using appliqué. We've used lots of inexpensive cotton fabrics for the appliqué trees, birds and border, and chosen a less fussy print for the background fabric. If necessary, you could simply turn a fabric over and use the wrong side of the cloth instead of the right side, as the pattern will be more delicate.*

The exciting part about making up this quilt is the fabric. All of the fabrics, apart from the background cloth, are scraps, the bits and pieces that you should have thrown out, but never did, and pieces of fabric sold as oddments in a remnant sale. If you are making the quilt for a new arrival in the family, you could even use fabrics that have some sentimental value, such as small scraps cut from a summer dress you wore when you were a young child, or your mother's old gingham pinafore.

Use the most elementary shapes for the design, such as simple bird

**You will need:**
Fabric for back and front: 2 pieces 60x90cm (24x36in)
Assorted fabric off-cuts
Gingham fabric: 2 strips 7.5x60cm (3x24in); 2 strips 7.5x90cm (3x36in)
Terylene wadding
Sewing thread and needle
Embroidery thread
Sewing machine
Iron
Scissors
Dressmaker's pins
Pencil
Brown paper
Tracing paper

  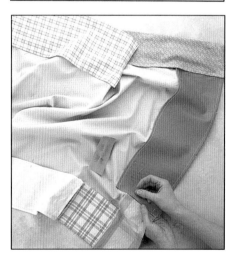

**1** *Select the fabrics for the quilt and assemble them together to make sure that the colours and patterns combine well. Some fabrics can be lightweight, some heavier, so long as they can all be washed in the same way and the colours will not run. Cut two rectangles of background fabric 60x90cm (24x36in) for the front and back of the baby quilt.*

**2** *Cut a variety of rectangles from smaller pieces of fabric to stitch around the edge of the front piece of the quilt to form an appliqué border. Sew the raw edges under, using a straight stitch on the machine or by hand, stitching as close to the turned edge as possible. Press the stitched pieces with an iron and trim away all the loose threads to neaten the edges.*

**3** *Pin the pieces around the edges of the front piece of fabric. Pin on the largest pieces first, then the smaller pieces, allowing some edges to overlap. Juggle them around until you are pleased with the overall effect. Place the pins into the fabric at right angles to the edges so that the machine can easily stitch over them. Use a zig-zag stitch to achieve a pretty effect.*

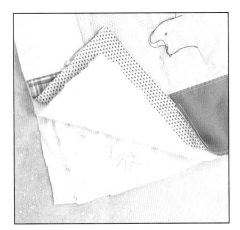

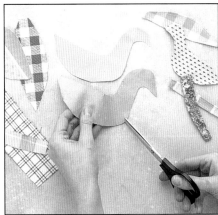

and leaf motifs. If some of the motifs become misshapen as you sew the raw edges under, then so much the better: this makes for a more interesting overall pattern and adds to the charm and character of the finished quilt.

## Machine or Hand Sew

Make sure that all the fabrics are compatible for washing together, and that none of the colours will run. A sewing machine makes the sewing of the quilt easier and much quicker, but it can be made entirely by hand if you wish.

Place a layer of terylene wadding between the top and bottom pieces of fabric; this gives the quilt a soft, padded look, and will make it warm and cosy for the baby. To secure the two layers of fabric and the wadding together, stitch a series of simple French knots, sewn using a contrasting embroidery thread.

**4** *Press the front and back pieces. Cut a piece of wadding to the same size and sandwich this between the two pieces of fabric. Keep the quilt flat on a table top, or on the floor, and secure the layers together with pins. Stitch simple French knots through all the thicknesses to hold together; we stitched about 20 inside the bordered area.*

**5** *Trace the appliqué motifs from the outlines provided and cut templates for each from brown paper. Pin these to scraps of fabric and cut out enough motifs to create an appliqué picture inside the bordered area. As you cut each piece, position it on the quilt until a picture builds up. Sew the raw edges under, and reposition on the quilt.*

## Pleasing Arrangement

The patchwork-effect border is sewn using odd-shaped rectangles of fabric. Sew the raw edges under each piece, then place these around the edge of the quilt, moving them around and overlapping some until you are happy with the arrangement. Pin, then stitch, each piece in place. The birds and tree shapes are attached in a similar manner: determine their positions by placing all the little pieces onto the fabric, then move them around until the design pleases you and stitch in place.

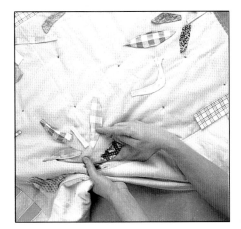

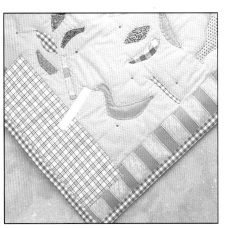

**6** *Pin the pieces onto the quilt, allowing some of the tree trunk shapes to overlap the bordered area to create interest. Snip away any loose threads from the appliqué shapes before you start to stitch them in place to avoid catching them with the sewing foot on the machine. Use zig-zag stitch to sew the shapes in place.*

**7** *Along each side of the quilt, sew on a 7.5cm (3in) strip of gingham fabric, 2.5cm (1in) from the outside edge, face down with the main width of fabric towards the centre of the quilt. Fold over to the other side of the quilt, enclosing all the raw edges, then turn a narrow hem under and use a straight stitch to close the edge. Hand stitch the corners.*

**Right:** *This pretty appliqué quilt will be warm and cosy for your baby, and it will be a joy to make, using inexpensive scraps and oddments of material. You can sew it by machine or by hand.*

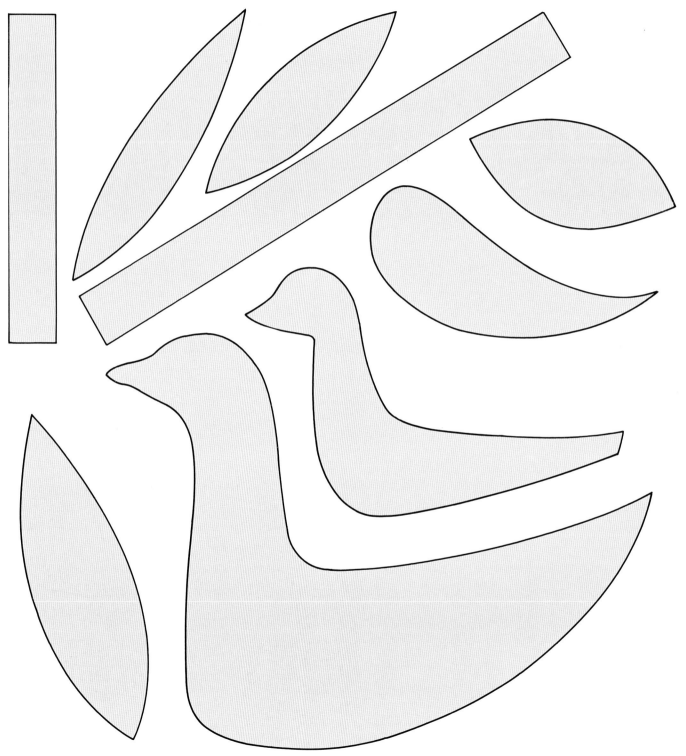

# GIRAFFE GROWTH CHART

*C*hildren will love to check their height against this lovable giraffe. Paint it with bright poster paints, sealing with a layer of varnish so that sticky finger marks can be wiped cleanly away.

**You will need:**
Plywood or hardboard 70x120cm (28x48in)
Paper tape measure and glue
Glass-paper
Fret saw
Decorator's and artist's brushes
White, yellow, brown and black emulsion paints
Pencil and rule
Varnish

This giraffe is made from a sheet of plywood or hardboard measuring 70x120cm (28x48in). If possible, get your supplier to cut a sheet to size for you; alternatively, look out for an offcut. As a last resort, buy a large sheet of wood and cut it down to size; there are many other projects in this book that can be made using the remainder of the sheet.

Enlarge the giraffe design onto the hardboard sheet using the simple grid system. Each square on the page represents 7.5cm (3in) on the board. Draw your grid onto the hard-board, then choose a point on the

**Right:** *This jolly, friendly giraffe will not only give your children an interest in checking their height, but will also provide a wonderful, colourful addition to the nursery.*

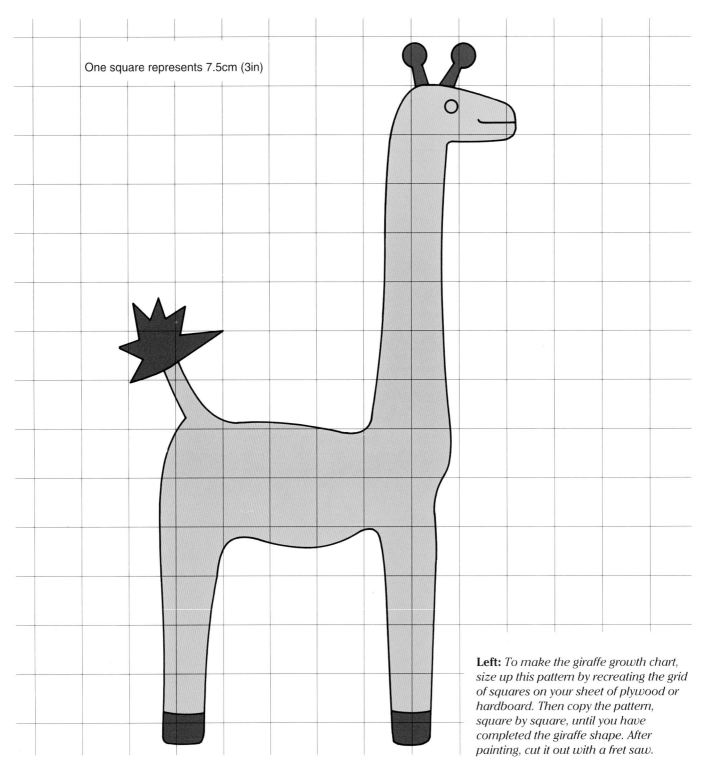

One square represents 7.5cm (3in)

**Left:** *To make the giraffe growth chart, size up this pattern by recreating the grid of squares on your sheet of plywood or hardboard. Then copy the pattern, square by square, until you have completed the giraffe shape. After painting, cut it out with a fret saw.*

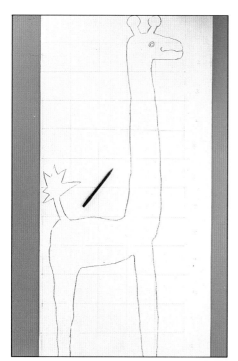

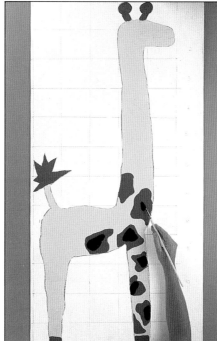

**1** *Prepare the hardboard or plywood by painting with two coats of white emulsion, allowing the first coat to dry before applying the second. Use a pencil to draw a 7.5x7.5cm (3x3in) grid onto the board. Draw the giraffe body on the board, using the grid as a reference, by copying the contents of each grid square. Copy the body first, then add legs, tail, neck and head.*

**2** *Paint the golden body colour first, using two coats of paint to achieve an even covering. Use an artist's brush to add large splodges of brown to make the giraffe markings, then add a smaller black centre to each. Any large shapes will suggest giraffe markings, but you can use our giraffe as a guide if you like. Paint the horns, hooves and top of the tail brown too.*

**3** *Cut the giraffe carefully from the board and use glass-paper to smooth the cut edges. Outline the shape with an even line of black paint, then paint the eye and a smiling mouth in black. Use glue to stick a tape measure in place, cutting it off at the giraffe's head. Seal the giraffe with two coats of varnish and stick it to the wall using sticky pads.*

pattern from which to start; we started with the body, then drew in the neck, legs and tail.

## Take Your Time

Follow the step-by-step instructions in the Introduction pages as a guide to using the fret saw to cut out the giraffe. It may take a little time to form the shape; cut small sections at a time, removing the excess board from the outside as you progress, allowing the saw blade to negotiate the corners. Don't worry if the blade

cuts beyond the outline at times, or even if it cuts inside the drawn line, as long as you keep the overall shape of the giraffe.

Glass-paper is used to smooth the edges, whether you are using hardboard or plywood. Plywood has a tendency to splinter quite easily, so sanding the edges is very important.

Any bright paint can be used for the giraffe, provided it is opaque enough to cover the grid marks. Emulsion or poster paints are the best, as they are very opaque and

your brushes can be washed out easily in water.

A layer of varnish will protect the painted finish. Acrylic varnish is convenient, as it is water-based and quick to dry, but you could use spray varnish. This may take a bit longer to dry, being spirit-based, but you will not need to clean any brushes.

Stick the giraffe over the skirting board or onto a door. If you place it above the skirting board, remember to adjust the position of the measurements on the tape accordingly.

# WINDOW STICKERS

*Children adore all kinds of stickers, and these seashore decorations will delight any small child. You could use the stickers to decorate most hard surfaces, but the light shining through the stickers on a window gives a stained-glass effect.*

**You will need:**
Tracing paper
Pencil
Paper and marker pen
Clear self-adhesive plastic
Coloured inks
Saucer or palette
Fine paint brush
Scissors

These decorations are painted onto self-adhesive plastic using coloured inks, which are available from craft shops in a variety of colours and are easy to use. If you have difficulty in finding these inks, you could use transparent glass paints, but don't be tempted to try any other paints or felt-tipped pens, as they will not adhere to the surface of the plastic and will peel or rub off.

Trace the seashore shapes from the pages and copy them onto a piece of paper. Cut each shape carefully from the plain paper and draw around the outline onto the self-adhesive plastic, using a marker pen. A small artist's brush is sufficient for painting in the colours, and the inks are easily washed away with water. You may find that the coloured inks tend to cover the plastic surface unevenly, leaving some dark and some light areas; this adds to the character of the stickers.

## Little Details
When the colours are completely dry, you will be able to paint in the black outlines and the little details, such as the fishes' eyes and fins and the starfish markings. To protect the coloured surfaces, it is advisable to

**Left:** *These seashore stickers are fun to make and look at. They will give an almost stained-glass effect when attached to a window in the nursery.*

stick another piece of plain self-adhesive plastic over the top of each shape and cut it to the same size. This will protect the colours and prevent them from cracking. It also makes window cleaning much easier, although they will not stand up to a lot of water.

## Use Your Own Designs
If these seashore motifs aren't quite to your liking, you can use the same technique for any decoration you

**1** *Trace around the seashore outlines and transfer these to a plain piece of paper. Cut around the outlines to produce a template for each shape. Use the templates to copy the shapes onto the self-adhesive plastic. Tip small amounts of coloured inks into a saucer or small palette and use them to colour each shape.*

may wish to have in the nursery. Use children's drawings as an alternative, or adapt a favourite character from a nursery rhyme or story. Make a tracing from the image in the same way as we show you here and copy the outline onto the self-adhesive plastic, then paint in the colours.

**2** *Leave the stickers to dry for a few minutes while you wash and dry the brush, then open the black ink. With a steady hand, use the black ink to paint in the outlines of the shapes to give them a definite edge. Then add the small details, such as the fishes' eyes inside the shapes, taking great care not to smudge the outline.*

21

**Below and right:** *Use these seashore shapes full size as patterns for the window stickers. Trace them from the pages, then copy them onto plain paper. Cut them out to make templates and use these to mark out the shapes on the clear self-adhesive plastic. Fill in the shapes with coloured inks, and paint in the outlines and details with black ink.*

**3** *When the shapes are dry, cut another piece of self-adhesive plastic large enough to fit over the motifs and cover them. Peel off the backing paper, and press the plastic over the painted shapes. Use a sharp pair of scissors to cut the shapes from the double layer of plastic, then peel off the backing paper and press onto the nursery window.*

# CHICKEN SHELF

*T*his jolly papier-mâché chicken is perched jauntily on top of a simple shelf unit. Its brightly-painted spots of colour bring a very special look to what would otherwise be plain, uninteresting shelves.

**You will need:**
Fine wire mesh
Wire cutters
Florist's wire
Newspaper
Wallpaper paste
Stiff card
White emulsion paint
Brush
Poster paints
Varnish
Strong adhesive
Shelf unit

Simple animal shapes such as this chicken are very easy to make from papier-mâché moulded around a wire mesh base. They look fabulous when painted with poster paints in strong primary colours.

Wire mesh is sold by hardware shops and DIY outlets, but look for places that sell short lengths, otherwise you will have to buy a whole roll. Cut out a rectangle, 30x60cm (12x24in), using wire cutters. Mould the mesh into a basic head and body shape; the wire needs to be compacted tightly to form the head, but can be left more open for the body. The tail is made by snipping the wire to form four long, thin finger shapes, which are twisted upwards to form the characteristic cockerel tail.

Roll a long, thin rectangle of mesh into a cigar shape and bend it to form a pair of legs. Secure them to the body with pieces of florist's wire.

Newspaper and wallpaper paste are the best materials for making papier-mâché. Tear long strips of newspaper before you begin pasting so that you can work the first layer quickly, as this can be difficult to

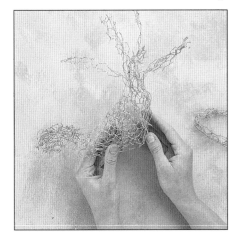

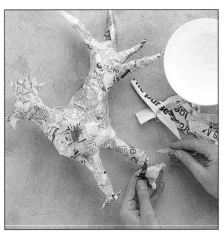

**1** *Bend and twist the wire mesh into a chicken shape. Use wire cutters or tinsnips to cut the four points that will form the chicken's tail and twist these upwards. Roll a 5x25cm (2x10in) piece of wire mesh into a cigar shape and bend it into a hairpin to form the legs. Secure the legs to the body with short lengths of florist's wire.*

**2** *Use strips of newspaper soaked with wallpaper paste to cover the chicken. When the first layer has been applied and allowed to dry, you can add the cockerel's comb and feet. Cut these shapes from stiff card and cover with a layer of paste and newspaper. Use more strips to stick these in place, apply a second layer and allow to dry.*

**3** *Continue the layering and drying process until at least five layers of papier-mâché have been applied. Allow the last layer to dry, then apply a coat of white emulsion paint. Once this is dry, you can begin painting with bright poster colours. Use your imagination to create your own eye-catching scheme, or copy our pattern of spots.*

**Right:** *An unusual papier-mâché chicken, painted in bright poster colours, will turn a simple set of shelves into a special piece of furniture.*

stick together. Apply the well-pasted strips around the wire frame like bandages, moulding the paper onto the wire with your hands. Apply at least five layers of paper, allowing each to dry out thoroughly before adding the next. This is time consuming, but you can speed drying by placing the chicken in a warm airing cupboard after applying each layer.

Once the chicken is dry, you can decorate it. We chose spots, but you could paint it with zig-zags or stripes, or cover a plain finish with stick-on stars. Apply two layers of spray-on varnish to protect the paint, allowing the first to dry before applying the second. Stick the chicken to the shelf unit with strong adhesive.

4 *Stand the chicken upright and place a weight across its feet to prevent it from falling over. This will allow you to apply spray-on varnish to the front and back of the chicken without getting sticky fingers. Apply two layers of varnish and, when they are completely dry, stick the chicken in position on the shelf, using a strong adhesive.*

# FLOOR MAT

*B*right and cheerful, this spotted floor mat will brighten up any nursery; and unlike a conventional mat or rug, it can be simply wiped clean, which is a useful feature where spillages are common. You can make the mat any size you prefer and finish it with any pattern you like.

This floor covering is inexpensive to make and can be painted to suit your own nursery's decor. We painted ours with a bold spotted design, which is easy to copy, but you may wish to co-ordinate the floor mat with the pattern on your wallpaper or paint it with a favourite nursery rhyme character. The designs are quickly sketched directly onto the fabric with an ordinary pencil, which can be rubbed out if you make a mistake, then painted using ordinary emulsion colours. The durability comes from the layers and layers of varnish that are applied once the paint is dry. Four or five layers are ideal and will produce a really hard-wearing mat.

## Cut Your Cloth

Ordinary canvas is the best material to use for the mat; it can be found in many art and craft shops, as it is the fabric artists use for painting their pictures. We used a piece measuring 91.5x145cm (36x57in), but you can cut your fabric according to the floorspace you have available. Turn a small hem, approximately 2.5cm (1in) wide, along all four sides of the canvas to neaten the edges. This could be stitched in place or stuck down with a general-purpose PVA adhesive.

Prepare the canvas by painting it with a layer of thinned white emulsion paint; you will need to really scrub into the close weave of the cloth with the bristles of the brush to obtain an even coverage. If you can, secure the four corners of the canvas while the emulsion layer dries, as this will help to prevent the sides of the cloth from wrinkling up. If the weather is fine, and you have the space; you could spread out the mat on a plastic sheet in the garden and place heavy weights on the corners. If you don't have the facility for this, do not worry unduly, as the cloth will eventually lie flat after a little wear and tear.

## A Crazed Pattern

The heavily-varnished layer of canvas has a tendency to crack underfoot, but don't be alarmed: this is quite acceptable. The fine cracks that are produced will form a crazed pattern that adds to the character of the mat.

A piece of self-adhesive felt attached to the underside of the canvas will cover all the ragged hems and produce a neater finish. If you cannot find self-adhesive felt to fit your mat, use a general-purpose adhesive to secure a piece of regular felt or cotton fabric as a backing. Remember to turn under the edges of a cotton backing to prevent them from fraying.

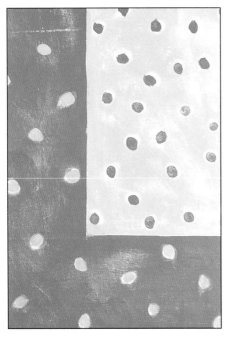

**Left:** *The spotted design we chose for our canvas mat is simple to apply. You can copy it exactly if you wish or use your own design.*

**Right:** *A colourful varnished canvas floor mat makes an attractive and practical feature for the nursery. It is easy to make and easy to keep clean.*

**1** Cut the canvas to the desired size, remembering to add 2.5cm (1in) all round for the hem. Glue the turnings underneath and paint the surface of the cloth with white emulsion thinned with an equal volume of water. Leave to dry, then use a pencil and rule to draw a deep border around the edges.

**2** Paint the area inside the border with a strong yellow emulsion paint. Use a small decorator's brush and almost scrub the paint onto the surface to create a distressed effect, rather than a flat, even layer. Rub away small areas of the yellow paint with a damp kitchen cloth to reveal spots of white paint.

**3** Paint in the border with blue emulsion, using the same scrubbing technique to apply a thin layer of colour and allowing some of the white paint to show through from underneath. Again, use the damp kitchen cloth to rub away small areas within the border to create the same spotted effect.

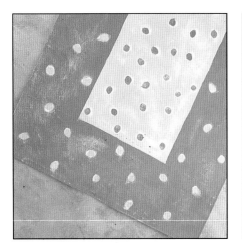

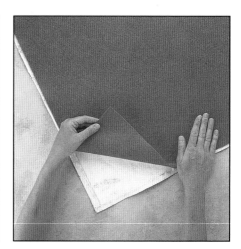

**4** Use an artist's brush to fill in the white spots with coloured emulsion. Use the same colours, but paint spots of blue on the yellow and spots of yellow on the blue. Don't allow the spots of colour to touch the background colour, but leave a small white halo around each for a pretty effect.

**5** When the paint is dry, apply a layer of varnish over the whole mat and allow to dry before applying another. Keep adding layers of varnish, allowing each to dry, until you have built up four or five layers. We used an acrylic floor varnish, as it is easy to use and the brushes can be washed in water.

**6** Cut a piece of self-adhesive felt to cover the back of the mat, making sure it covers all the ragged edges. Press one corner of the felt in place and pull the backing paper off gradually, smoothing the felt over the mat as you go to ensure perfect adhesion with no trapped air bubbles or unsightly creases.

# Paper Wall Border

*Rather than buying a ready-made wallpaper border for the nursery, why not simply make your own from children's drawings? You will only need four or five different drawings, which can be photocopied as many times as you like to run all the way around the room, or simply along the back of a shelf; it's up to you.*

This border is so much more attractive, and certainly more unique, than anything you could buy in a shop, and it's also a great way of using the beautiful drawings that children can produce. We have copied a row of houses for this border, but you may choose to copy drawings of flowers, cars, animals or anything that your child likes to draw. If your child is too small to produce recognizable drawings, you could always try to emulate this naïve style yourself by drawing a picture with the pencil held in your left hand if you are right-handed, or your right if left-handed. This can produce very convincing results.

## How Many Copies?

Use A4 sheets of paper and encourage your child to draw a selection of houses or animals, or whatever theme you are looking for, so that each drawing will fill most of a sheet. If you intend to run the border all around the walls of the nursery, use a retractable tape to measure the distance you intend to cover, then divide this measurement by the width of your paper to give you the total number of copies that you will need.

The drawings are stuck to the wall using wallpaper paste; follow the mixing instructions on the packet to make sure you obtain a smooth, lump-free texture. Brush the paste onto each print and position it on the wall. It is important to smooth the print onto the wall by pressing your hand from the centre of the print outwards, pushing out any air bubbles that may be trapped underneath the paper.

## Fun to Paint

Colouring the border should be fun: do it yourself or let your child do it. Either way, use a thick paint brush to produce a delightful childish style. Use thinned water colours or poster paints and don't worry about painting over the outlines occasionally, as this adds to the charm of the border.

If your paint is too thick, you will obliterate the black outlines, but if it is too thin, it may start to run down the walls. Experiment on an inconspicuous section of the border first, such as the area behind a door, until you are happy with the consistency of the paint. Restrict yourself to the strong primary colours for a more eye-catching border.

## A Protective Finish

The border can be sealed by applying a layer of acrylic varnish if you like, which will allow sticky finger marks to be wiped off relatively easily. However, this is optional and it may make the border difficult to remove at a later date.

1 *Select the drawings that are to be printed; the border will look more effective if the houses are of slightly different sizes, as this will add character to a long section. Measure the wall to calculate the number of copies you will need. Print an equal number of each drawing. Keep the originals aside, as the ink may run when painted over.*

**Overleaf:** *What better way of displaying your child's drawings than to copy them and turn them into a border for the nursery. Fix them to the wall with wallpaper paste and paint them with bright poster colours.*

**2** *Lay out the drawings on a table as you would like them to look on the wall. It looks effective if the houses have a 'street' feel to them, so cut away any deep edges that have no details drawn on them. Do not cut any paper off the top or bottom of the sheet, as the border looks best if it has an even height.*

**3** *Use a spirit level and a pencil to draw a horizontal line all around the room. Mix the wallpaper paste and paste up each print, aligning it with the pencil line. Position the prints carefully to keep the border straight. Smooth each print from the centre outwards and allow to dry overnight.*

**4** *Once the border is dry, it can be painted, using thinned poster paints or water colours for the best results. Use a fat brush for a simple paint style; allow a child to colour some or all of the border if they wish. Paint in the walls first along the whole border, then the roofs, varying the colours as you go.*

**5** *Paint in the smaller details last, but still with the fat brush. It adds to the naïve charm if the curtains are dashed in roughly with one stroke of the brush. Flowers are added in the same way. Once the border is finished and completely dry, it may be given a coat of acrylic varnish to seal and protect it.*

# Noah's Ark Wallhanging

*T*his colourful wallhanging will cheer up the nursery as well as provide a stimulating activity toy. The animals are removable: one from each pair fits neatly into a felt pocket, while the other has a Velcro tab stitched to its back, allowing it to be fixed to the ark itself.

**You will need:**
Tracing paper
Pencil
Brown paper
Dressmaker's pins
Red felt: 42x70cm (17x28in)
Ginger felt: 25x32cm (10x13in)
Beige felt: 27x32cm (11x13in)
Off-cuts of navy, chocolate, white,
  yellow and grey felts for pockets
  and animals
Thread
Toy stuffing
Needle
String
Embroidery thread
Fabric glue
Scissors
Velcro pads

Begin by enlarging the patterns, using the grid technique outlined in the Introduction to form templates for each section of the ark. We used a double thickness of felt for the ark pieces; this not only enabled us to form a pocket for the giraffe, but it also gave a padded quality to the finished design. Felt is the ideal material to use, as it does not fray at the edges once cut and it is available in lots of brilliant colours.

Cut out all the sections of the ark,

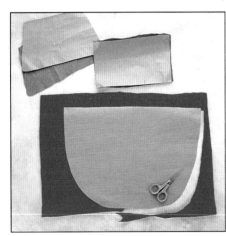

**1** *Scale-up the ark shapes, using the instructions in the Introduction, and transfer onto brown paper; cut out the resulting full-size templates. Pin the templates to the felt squares and cut out the two layers of felt for each of the ark pieces. Trace the animal shapes onto offcuts of felt and cut these out carefully.*

using a different coloured felt for each part. We used conventional colours, such as the red hull and two-tone brown cabin, but don't be restricted by this. There's no reason why you shouldn't have a purple hull with an orange and yellow boathouse, for example.

## A Quick Project

If you have a sewing machine, it takes no time at all to sew around the boat pieces, but this project can still be made by hand. All you need to do is stitch the pieces together with a short running stitch, using threads which match the different coloured felts.

The animals are stitched together entirely by hand because they are so small. Stuff all the shapes with a small amount of filling to give a more rounded appearance. The markings are either sewn or stuck on; little pieces of string make amusing tails, while the smaller features, such as the eyes, are stitched with a simple French knot.

It is important to use very close, straight stitches to form the zebra stripes. Make the stitches very short at the beginning of each stripe, then make them progressively longer, finally tapering again towards the end. Repeat this arrangement five or six times across the zebra's body on one thickness of felt only, then sew the two sides together, adding a little

stuffing before you close the shape. The remaining animals can be sewn and filled first: their markings are added last.

## A Permanent Place

If you have a permanent position in mind for the wallhanging, use self-adhesive Velcro to secure the ark to the wall. One part of the Velcro is stuck to the wall and the other to the back of the wallhanging. Stitch the Velcro to the latter for extra security, as the adhesive backing may not adhere particularly well to the soft, fluffy felt.

**Right:** *This delightful wallhanging with its rich colours and cuddly animals will not only brighten up the nursery, but also provide your child with a wonderful toy. The tiny soft animals are easily removed from the ark for play, but can be kept safe when not in use.*

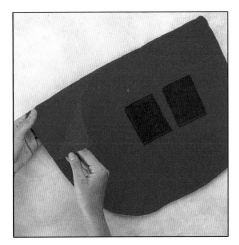

**2** *Pin, then stitch, two small rectangles of blue felt onto a single layer of the red felt hull to form pockets for an elephant and a giraffe. Sew around the curved edge of the two boat hull pieces, keeping the stitching as close to the edge as possible and leaving the straight edge open; repeat with the roof pieces.*

**3** *Sew a pocket onto one layer of the boathouse section, then sew all four sides of the two boathouse pieces together. Slot the boathouse inside the two layers of roof and the two hull pieces, sewing the two openings closed to secure. Remember to leave a small pocket open for the giraffe.*

**4** *The animal pieces should be sewn together using blanket stitch (see page 45) and matching thread. Stuff the animals lightly before closing the seams. Sew the lion's legs together, then slot them between the head pieces as they are being sewn together. Sew the ears in place and fix a string tail on the elephant.*

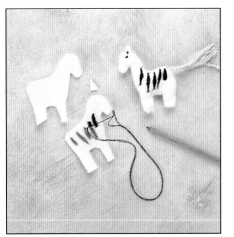

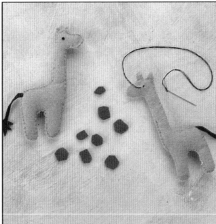

**5** *The zebra's stripes are stitched onto the body before sewing the pieces together; use a pencil to mark the stripes and follow the progression of stitches outlined on page 32. Sew the body together, stuffing lightly, then add the ears and a string tail. Separate the strands of string to make the tail bushy.*

**6** *Sew an eye onto each animal, using a single French knot and black embroidery thread. Stick on the giraffe's markings using fabric glue, then sew on a felt tail. Sew Velcro pads onto the backs of one giraffe, elephant, lion and zebra, and the corresponding pads onto the ark. Stick the animals in place.*

**Right:** *Trace these full-size shapes of the ark's animals and use the tracings to make brown paper or cardboard templates. Use these to mark and cut out the animal shapes on offcuts of felt. Then cut out two shapes for each animal. Stuff the animals lightly, as you sew them together, as this will give them a more rounded appearance. Their various markings can be sewn or stuck on as desired.*

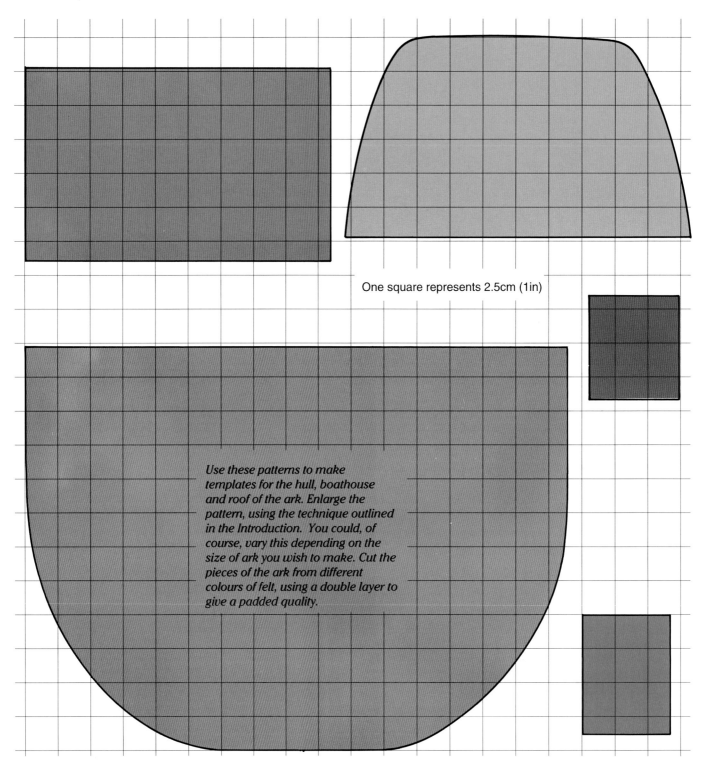

One square represents 2.5cm (1in)

*Use these patterns to make
templates for the hull, boathouse
and roof of the ark. Enlarge the
pattern, using the technique outlined
in the Introduction. You could, of
course, vary this depending on the
size of ark you wish to make. Cut the
pieces of the ark from different
colours of felt, using a double layer to
give a padded quality.*

# PRETTY PICTURE FRAME

*It is stimulating for any baby or small child to have lots of brightly-coloured pictures displayed around the nursery. This inexpensive picture frame is easily made from an ordinary cardboard box and can be practically any size you care to make it, for anything from a small photograph to a full sheet of patterned wrapping paper.*

Often, it is the most simple and elementary shapes that catch the eye, and the basic flower motif that decorates this picture frame couldn't be simpler. Cut lots of flowers from off-cuts of card, tracing the shape from the page, and stick them around the basic frame. We used a tube of general-purpose glue to create a heart motif between each of the flowers; the bead of glue soon dries to form an interesting relief pattern that can be carefully painted.

## Protecting the Picture
Thin strips of card have been used between the front and back pieces of the frame to act as spacers, forming a gap into which you can slide the picture. If you want the picture or print to be protected, then cut a sheet of acetate or thick plastic to the same size as the picture and slide it in front of the picture inside the frame. It can easily be wiped clean with a cloth or duster, but is a fraction of the weight of a piece of glass. This type of material is often used for cutting stencils, so it can be purchased in many craft shops, as well as stationery shops as it is used to protect maps, prints and diagrams. It can be easily cut to size with the aid of a craft knife or a sharp pair of scissors.

Once the frame is assembled, seal and protect the surface with two coats of varnish. This gives the frame a rich, glossy finish and strengthens it slightly.

## Display Options
If you want to display the picture frame on the wall of the nursery, secure two brass rings to the back with tape and tie a piece of string or picture wire between them. If the frame is to be stood on a shelf or table, however, you will need to cut out a triangular support from an off-cut of card, and tape this to the back of the frame.

**You will need:**
Corrugated cardboard
Pencil and ruler
Craft knife
Scissors
Tracing paper
General-purpose glue
Scrap paper
Decorator's brush
Artist's brush
Blue/green emulsion paint
Yellow poster paint
Varnish

**Below:** *This simple picture frame has been decorated with an equally-simple relief pattern of flowers and hearts. The flowers are cut from cardboard and stuck in place; the hearts are formed by squeezing out beads of glue.*

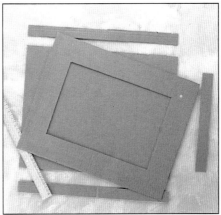

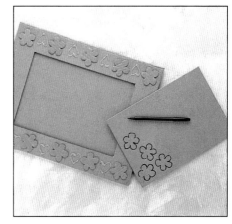

**1** Cut two rectangles from corrugated card, making them 15cm (6in) wider and deeper than the picture. Our picture measured 15x25cm (6x10in), so we made the frame 30x40cm (12x16in). Draw a 7.5cm (3in) border inside one of the rectangles and cut out the centre to leave an even frame. Cut three 2.5cm (1in) strips of card to act as spacers.

**2** Trace the template from the page and use it to cut the flower motifs. We used 14 flowers to decorate this frame. Glue the spacer strips to the front of the solid piece of card, along one side and the top and bottom edges. Stick the frame to the spacers. Glue the flowers to the front of the frame and use more glue to draw a heart between each pair.

**Above:** Trace this full-size pattern to make a template for the flower shapes, cutting them out from offcuts of corrugated cardboard.

**Left:** Pretty pictures always have a place in the nursery, whether they be photographs, your child's drawings, prints, or simply sections of colourful wallpaper or wrapping paper. This easily-made picture frame provides a pretty surround to match.

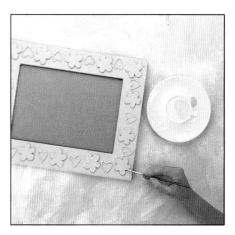

**3** Slide scrap paper inside the frame to protect the centre, then paint the front, back and edges with two coats of emulsion. Use a second colour and a fine brush to outline the edge of each flower and to highlight the heart shapes. Choose colours to complement the decor of your nursery. Finally, use an acrylic varnish to protect the frame.

# WOODLAND COAT HANGERS

*Making these wooden animal shapes is great fun; once you have mastered the cutting technique with the fret saw, you'll be cutting out lots of these delightful creatures. As well as gluing the animals onto children's coat hangers, you could make a mobile by simply drilling a hole in the top of each and threading them with fishing line.*

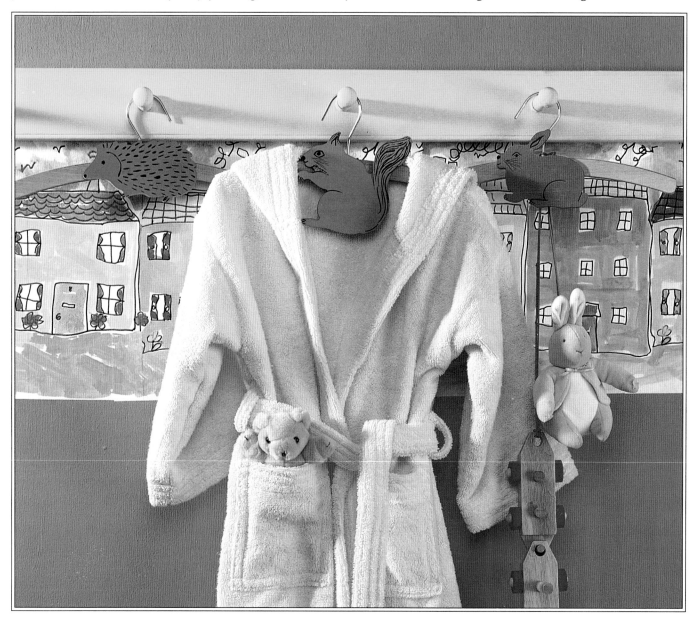

**You will need:**
Tracing paper
Pencil
Plywood
Fret saw
Glass-paper
Poster paints
Brush
Strong adhesive
Wooden coat hangers

We have used a piece of plywood to make the animals for this project. Plywood can be bought from most hardware and DIY stores, but look for small offcuts, otherwise you will have to buy a whole sheet, which will be quite large. Trace the animal shapes from the page and transfer each onto the plywood, then cut around the shape with a fret saw, following the simple instructions in the Introduction.

## A Helping Hand

If you are not used to working with a fret saw, you may find it easier with the help of a friend. Have them hold the plywood flat on the edge of the table and rotate it slowly as you cut. This will enable you to concentrate on cutting without having to turn the wood; cutting will be easier if you avoid stopping the blade mid-way.

Use poster paints for the animals, painting some in their natural colours - like the brown mole - but allowing your imagination to play a part with others, such as the blue hedgehog and green squirrel. Apply dashes of black paint to the shapes to suggest the animals' eyes, noses, whiskers and other character details.

## Avoiding Splits

Remember to use wooden hangers that have been specially designed for children's clothes. We found that a strong glue was sufficient to fix the wooden shapes onto the hangers. Avoid using screws or nails which could split the wood of either the hangers or the animals themselves.

**Left:** *Even the most utilitarian of objects in the nursery can be given a sense of fun, such as these wooden coat hangers. By attaching a brightly-coloured wooden animal to the front of each hanger, you can turn them into practical items that your child will love to use. At the same time, he or she will learn the importance of keeping clothes tidy.*

**Overleaf:** *Trace the full-size patterns of the animals on page 42 and copy them onto plywood so that you can cut out the shapes with a fret saw. After sanding, paint the shapes jolly colours, using the patterns as a guide for painting the various character details on the animals, such as eyes, noses and so on.*

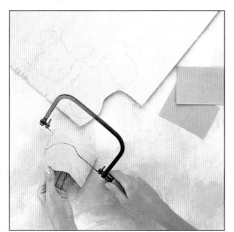

**1** *Transfer the animal shapes onto the plywood. Be economical with the sheet by turning each shape to fill gaps and make the best use of the wood. Cut out each animal roughly from the sheet, then cut carefully around the outline for the correct shape. Use fine glass-paper to sand the edges until very smooth.*

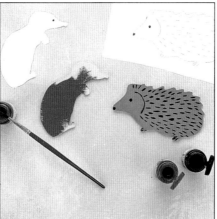

**2** *Use poster colours to paint the shapes, choosing strong shades. Remember to paint the front and back, as some parts of the animals may be visible from both sides. Once the base colour is dry, use the patterns as a guide to painting in the character details on the front in black. Leave to dry.*

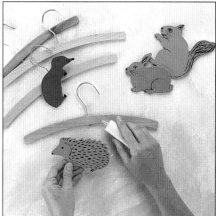

**3** *Use a strong adhesive to glue an animal to the front of each wooden coat hanger. Wait until the glue has set before putting any clothes onto the hanger. Test the strength of the adhesive by giving the wooden animals a sharp tug. If they stay firmly in place, the glue is sufficiently dry.*

# POP-UP PUPPETS

*This is a new working of a traditional toy. We have used modern air-drying clay for the animal heads and bright felts for the bodies. Tiny babies will be enchanted at the 'now you see me, now you don't' action of these toys if you work the puppets for them, while slightly older children will find hours of pleasure inventing their own stories for the pop-up characters.*

Moulding the animal heads for these pop-up puppets from air-drying clay is actually much simpler than it may first appear, and you can make any animals you like. This useful material can be purchased from most art and craft shops.

## Where to Start

Begin by using your fingers to mould and squeeze a small lump of clay - about the size of a golf ball - into a rough sphere. Pull a little of the clay down at the bottom to form a neck, then tease out the nose and ears, using your fingertips. Shape these features according to the animal you are making; for example, squash the nose a little to form a flat end for a piglet snout, or leave it pointed to make a convincing fox nose.

Before the clay has a chance to dry out, push the end of the length of doweling into the neck of the animal head to form a socket. Then remove the doweling carefully, trying not to enlarge the hole too much, as the wooden rod will be glued back into it later.

## Fit to the Cone

When you are fashioning the head from the clay, bear in mind that the whole head and the fabric body should be able to slide in and out of the cone with ease. The simplest way of making sure that this can be achieved is to roll up the base cone at the same time as forming the head, and keep checking the size of the head against the size of the cone's opening.

We used a lightweight cardboard to make the cone, as this is strong enough to withstand the rough treatment that it will undoubtedly receive from its young users, yet flexible enough to be rolled smoothly into a conical shape.

## The Perfect Material

Felt is the perfect material for the puppet bodies, as it will not fray at the edges, but if you would rather make the toys from a patterned fabric instead, remember to turn under all the raw edges as hems. Simple blanket stitch is used to stitch the two halves of each body together, while the paw or hoof markings can be drawn onto the felt with the aid of a tube of fabric paint with a pointed nozzle. However, if you prefer, you could use an embroidery thread instead.

All sorts of decorative touches can be added to these puppets, such as buttons running down the fronts of the bodies or lace trimmings around the top edges of the cones. Whatever extra trimmings you decide to add, remember that they must be very secure so that little fingers cannot pull them off.

**1** *Pull a small lump of clay from the pack and mould it into an animal head, as described in the text, using your fingers. Pull a portion of it downwards to fashion the neck. Cut a piece of doweling to a length of about 50cm (20in). Push the doweling upwards through the neck and well into the head, then stroke the wet clay around the rod before gently removing it.*

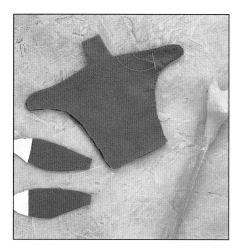

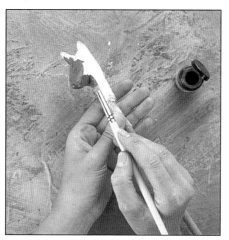

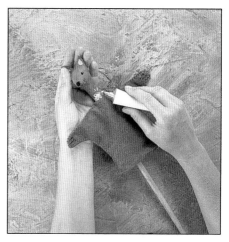

**2** When the head is dry, glue the doweling into its socket with a strong adhesive. Cut out the body of the animal, using the grid technique. Choose the colour of the felt to suggest the animal you are making: a pink pig or a brown fox. Sew the body together, leaving the neck and base open.

**3** Paint the head using poster paints, allowing the base colour to dry thoroughly before adding the features with a fine brush. Use black dots to suggest the eyes and nose, a little pink triangle to give detail to the ear, a happy smile and a few smart whiskers to suggest the character of this jolly fox.

**4** Use a strong adhesive to glue the felt body onto the neck. Thread the body onto the doweling and apply glue around the clay neck area. Roll the felt collar underneath while pushing the body upwards so that the cut edge of the felt lies inside the body. Add the paw or hoof details with fabric paint or thread.

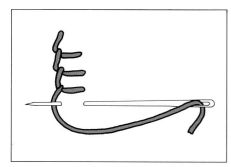

**Above:** When you are ready to sew the two sections of each felt animal body together, use simple blanket stitch, as illustrated.

**Left:** Children of all ages will love these colourful pop-up animal puppets. The very young will be enthralled to watch as you make them pop in and out of their cones, while older children will enjoy inventing their own adventures for the little animals.

**5** If you are making a fox, cut out a tail, using the template provided, including the two white tips. The tail is sewn in the same way as the body, the white triangles being sewn on top of the brown felt at the end of the tail. Stuff the tail lightly with a little toy stuffing, then use overstitches to secure it to the body.

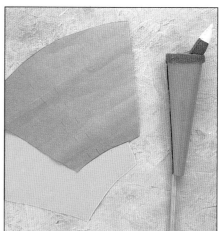

**6** Make a paper pattern for the cone and cut the shape from card. Roll it up, using glue to secure. Thread the cone onto the doweling and glue the base of the body around the top of the cone. Cut out a piece of self-adhesive felt, using the cone pattern, and stick onto the card to cover the untidy edges.

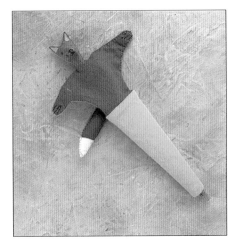

**7** *Varnish the clay head, using polyurethane or water-based varnish to protect the surface. If you wish to add any further decoration to the body, make sure that it is firmly attached before allowing children to use the puppet. If you cut the doweling rod to length with a saw, you will need to sand the end smooth to prevent the risk of splintering.*

**Right:** *To make the puppet bodies and base cone, scale-up these patterns, using the grid technique described in the Introduction. Draw your grids on paper and cut out the resulting patterns to act as templates for cutting the felt bodies and lightweight card and felt cones.*

One square represents 2.5cm (1in)

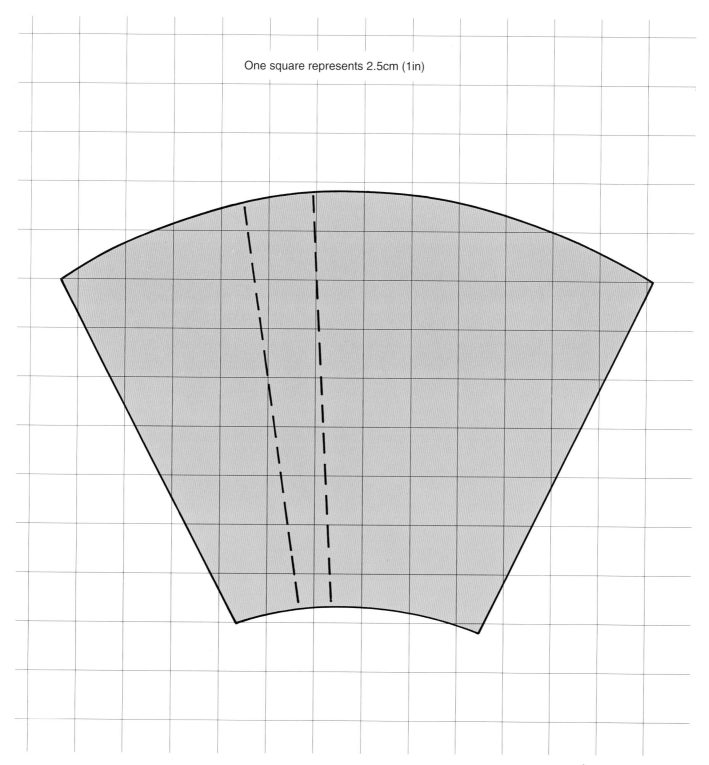

One square represents 2.5cm (1in)

# FARMYARD MOBILE

*Mobiles are stimulating for young babies, particularly if hung above a cot, as they will rotate in the slightest movement of air and attract the child's attention. These familiar farmyard animals are shapes that the baby will soon recognize as it begins to grow up and develop learning skills.*

**You will need:**
Tracing paper
Pencil and paper
Needle and thread
Rule
Scissors
Selection of felt off-cuts
Fabric glue
Black fabric paint
Silver jewellery rings
Fishing line
Doweling: 1 length 23cm (9in),
    1 length 18cm (7in) and 1 length
    12.5cm (5in)
Glass-paper
Blue poster paint
Screw-in eyelet
String or ribbon

The beauty of felt is that it won't fray and it comes in a rainbow of bright colours. These wonderful farmyard animals are cut from squares of felt and are made by sticking two of the shapes together, using fabric glue. Fabric paint is used to add the eyes, noses and all the other small details, although you can stitch these with embroidery thread if you prefer.

The animals are suspended from short pieces of painted doweling, using clear fishing line. Because the weights of your animals may differ from ours, tie them loosely onto the

doweling in the positions we have suggested, then hold the mobile in the air. If it hangs at an angle, move the fishing line supports along the rods to correct the balance of the animals. When the rods are hanging level, secure the animals in position by dabbing a little glue onto each piece of fishing line where it wraps around the rod.

If you want a larger mobile for an older child's room, simply scale-up the animal templates using the grid technique or a photocopier and hang from longer pieces of doweling.

**Right:** *These farmyard animals, bobbing about with the slightest air movement, will captivate your baby.*

**1** *Trace the animal shapes and transfer to paper. Cut out the shapes and use as patterns for the felt pieces. Some animals can be cut from several different felt colours, such as yellow for the duck's body and orange for its feet.*

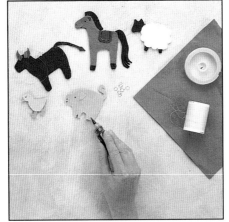

**2** *Glue two sides of each animal together, inserting the sheep head and legs, and the duck legs inside the body pieces. Use fine-lining fabric paint to draw in the features. Sew a silver ring to each animal and thread with fishing line.*

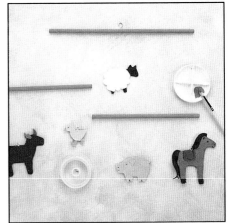

**3** *Cut three pieces of doweling to length and smooth the ends with glass-paper; paint with poster colour. String up the mobile as shown on page 50, screw a small eyelet into the longest piece of doweling and thread with ribbon.*

**Below:** *Use this diagram as a guide to assembling the mobile. Make sure the dowels are level when the mobile is supported from its central string - adjust the positions of the animals if necessary.*

**Right:** *Use these full-size patterns to make templates for the felt farmyard animals. Cut two pieces of felt for the main body of each animal and sandwich features such as ears, legs and tails between them. If you want a larger mobile, scale-up the patterns using the grid technique.*

# CLOWN STORAGE BOX

*This cheerful decorated box can be used for all kinds of things, from a container to hide an uninteresting box of nappy wipes to a handy storage bin for small toys and games. However you decide to make use of the box, it will make a delightful accessory for any nursery.*

**You will need:**
Corrugated cardboard
Craft knife or scissors
Ruler
Newspaper
Wallpaper paste
Gummed paper
White emulsion paint
Decorator's brush
Pencil
Coins
Poster paints
Artist's brush
Varnish

This colourful box, with its smiling clown handle, can be made entirely from bits and pieces that you are likely to have laying around. Cardboard salvaged from a grocery box and a few old newspapers are transformed into the bright container. It is very simple to make, using the old-fashioned method of papier-mâché that many of us will have learned at school.

The basic cardboard structure is made and held together with strips of gummed paper. Then about four layers of newspaper are used to cover the box. These will dry hard to provide a really tough structure, which can be boldly painted with bright poster paints. It really couldn't be easier.

## A Clown Handle

Our smiling clown is formed from a double thickness of thin card, stuck together and fed through a slot in the box lid. The two flaps at the base

**Right:** *This cheery and brightly-patterned clown box is easy to make from scraps of card and makes a very versatile accessory for the nursery.*

**1** *You will need a base, four sides and a lid cut from corrugated cardboard. The lid and base should both be slightly larger than the box itself to make an overhang. To prevent the lid from sliding off, cut a piece of card slightly smaller than the box and glue it to the underside of the lid.*

**2** *Use strips of gummed paper to hold the pieces of card together. Then start to apply the first layer of newspaper, using wallpaper paste to stick the strips in place. Once you have completed a layer, allow it to dry before applying the next. Put the box in a warm place to accelerate drying.*

**3** *Build up at least four layers of papier-mâché, allowing each layer to dry thoroughly, until you have formed a solid structure. Paint the inside and outside of the box with two coats of ordinary white emulsion paint to hide the newsprint. Then set the box aside until the paint has dried.*

of the clown are folded back and glued to the undersides of the lid. Layers of wallpaper paste and newspaper built up on the lid will ensure that the clown handle remains firmly in position.

A layer of varnish will seal and protect the box from any misuse. A water-based acrylic varnish is convenient for this, as the brush you use can be washed out in water afterwards, but a polyurethane varnish will also have the desired effect if you prefer.

## Sizing It Up

Size up your box according to the intended use. If it is going to hold a box of moist wipes, for example, cut the pieces to the size of that container, leaving a 5cm (2in) margin all round. In fact, you can make the box any size you like, but bear in mind the size of the clown handle.

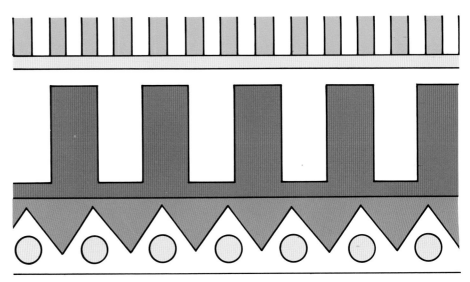

**Above:** *You can decorate the clown box with a geometric pattern of bright colours, such as the one shown here. Use a pencil and rule to draw out the* pattern on the sides and top, adjusting it to suit the size of the box. Alternatively, you could apply a more random pattern of spots or splashes of colour.

**4** *Use a pencil and ruler to draw a bold pattern on the surface of the box, either following our design or making up your own simple geometric scheme. Use coins as templates for the circles of colour. Paint the patterns on the box, using bright poster paint in primary colours.*

**5** *Cut the clown from two layers of card and bind the pieces together with papier-mâché, leaving the two lower flaps uncovered. Build up four layers of paper as before, paint with emulsion, then poster colours. Cut a 10cm (4in) slit centrally in the lid of the box using a craft knife.*

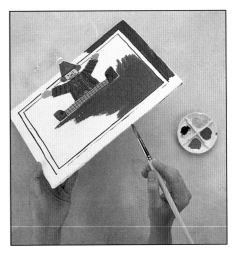

**6** *Push the clown through the slit, fold back the base flaps and glue them to the underside of the lid. Paint the lid of the box with the clown in position, using bold patterns and strong primary colours. Protect and seal the box by applying two layers of varnish, allowing the first to dry before adding the second.*

**Right:** *Use this full-size pattern as a guide for cutting out the clown handle. Trace it from the page and copy the tracing onto thin card. Cut out two clown shapes and glue them back to back to form the handle. Cover the clown with papier-mâché and secure to the box by bending back the base flaps and gluing them to the underside of the lid.*

# NAPPY SACK

*This pretty broderie anglaise sack is designed to hold a stack of unsightly nappies and can be tied to a hook or onto the edge of the cot with its broad satin ribbon. The nappies are easily reached through the flap at the front of the sack without having to undo any tricky fastenings.*

This nappy sack is easily made from four rectangles of fabric, two of which form a rigid base with a piece of card inside to keep it flat. The top of the sack is folded over to form a channel through which satin ribbon is threaded. We chose a pretty fabric for our sack because it complements the fabric canopy of the cot. You could choose a boldly-patterned fabric if you prefer, or add an appliqué motif for a different effect.

As nappies vary in size, becoming larger as the child grows, we used the dimensions of the largest nappy, plus a little extra all round. So although newborn baby nappies may seem quite small in the holder, the largest ones will fit perfectly. The flap at the front means that there are no buttons or zips to unfasten, making a busy parent's chore a little easier.

We used a frilled lace edging to decorate the sack. This softens the edges a little and is easily added by hand, using basic overstitch.

**You will need:**
Fabric: 1 piece 60x125cm (24x50in) and 3 pieces 33x21cm (13x8¼in)
Pins
Corrugated cardboard
Scissors
150cm (60in) of 2.5cm (1in) wide ribbon
Large threading needle
Needle and thread
170cm (68in) of lace edging

**Right:** *This pretty broderie anglaise nappy sack, with its delicate lace trimming, makes a practical addition to the nursery. It will hold several nappies so that they are readily to hand, the ingenious front flap making them easy to reach when needed.*

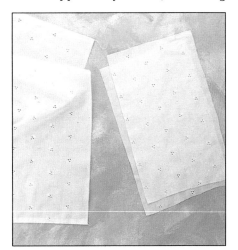

**1** *Start by cutting the pieces from the fabric. You will need one large rectangular piece to form the sides, and three base pieces: one to form the actual base of the sack and two to form an envelope into which the cardboard base will slide.*

**2** *Sew a narrow hem along all four sides of the large rectangle. Pin one of the long edges, right sides facing, around all four sides of a base piece, creating the double flap by overlapping it across one of the longer edges of the base. Sew in place.*

**3** *Turn the sack right sides out and fold over a 5cm (2in) hem at the top of the sack, towards the inside, to create a channel for the ribbon. Pin this edge evenly, then sew all the way around, using a straight stitch by hand or on a sewing machine.*

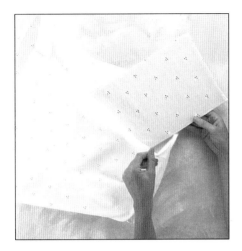

**4** *Sew the two remaining base pieces together, right sides facing, around three sides, using the smallest hem you can. Turn right sides out and cut a piece of corrugated card to fit neatly inside; hand stitch the fourth side closed. Slot this base inside the nappy sack.*

**5** *Cut a neat V-shape into the ends of a 150cm (60in) length of 2.5cm (1in) wide ribbon and thread onto a large, blunt needle. Pass the needle through the channel in the top of the nappy sack and tie the two free ends of ribbon into a neat bow after removing the needle.*

**6** *Hand stitch a piece of lace edging right around the base section of the nappy sack and another along the edge of the front flap for a pretty finish. Simply hang the sack up by the satin ribbon and pass the nappies in and out through the opening at the front.*

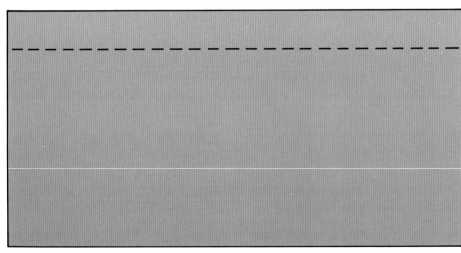

125cm (50in)

60cm (24in)

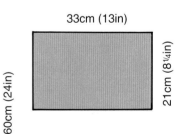

33cm (13in)

21cm (8¼in)

*Use these dimensions for cutting the fabric for the nappy sack. You need one large piece for the main part of the sack and three smaller pieces for the bottom. Two of these are sewn together and contain a piece of corrugated card to act as a stiffener. The main piece should have a large hem turned over at the top for the ribbon.*

# DECORATIVE AQUARIUM

*This wonderful seascape aquarium makes a colourful and unusual nursery decoration. It is easily converted from a cardboard grocery box, while the dangling fishes started life as plastic soft drinks bottles. We cut a comb from a scrap of card and used this to pull through the wet paint on the outside of the aquarium to form the pretty wave pattern.*

**Below:** *Bring the wonders of the ocean to your nursery with this fascinating aquarium, complete with its colourful fish. A seagull perched on top and a toy sailboat provide finishing touches.*

**You will need:**
Cardboard box
Stiff card offcuts
Scissors
Pencil
Newspaper
Wallpaper paste
White and blue emulsion paints
Decorator's brush
Plastic soft drinks bottles
Stapler or paper clips
Coloured tissue papers
Poster paints and artist's brush
String
Needle
Glue
Sharp knife or hacksaw

When making this aquarium, look for a suitable cardboard box in the supermarket; the size can vary according to how large you want to make it. This medium-sized box has enough space to hold three fishes, but you may prefer to make an oceanic display, in which case you will need a larger box and a vivid imagination!

## A Strong Box

A simple wave shape is cut from thin card and pasted onto the box with newspaper strips and wallpaper paste, using the papier-mâché technique. Employ the same technique to build up three layers of paper all over the box, inside and outside, so that it will be strong enough to withstand the rigours of the nursery.

We used simple methods to decorate the aquarium. These included combing and a paint splatter effect to suggest the foaming crests of the sea's waves.

## Little Fishes

The best part of this project is making the delightful little fishes. We used individual plastic soft drinks bottles for the small fishes, and a large bottle for the biggest fish. You will need a sharp craft blade or a saw with fine teeth, such as a hacksaw, to cut off the screw section of the bottle neck, leaving a hard plastic ring that forms the fish's open mouth. The rest of the bottle can easily be cut to shape, using a pair of sharp scissors.

Bright tissue papers are layered over the plastic bottles creating the striking fish colours. On the largest fish, we used two different colours; don't worry if the colours begin to run slightly, as this will not spoil the effect of the fish. You will need to hold the tail section together with paper clips or staples as you apply the glued tissue paper. These can be removed once the paper has dried. Black poster paint is used to paint in the eyes.

Use nylon fishing line or thin string to suspend the fishes in their aquarium, varying the length so that the fishes are placed at different heights. The string is threaded through holes pierced in the roof of the aquarium and held securely with large knots on the top.

## Decorate with Shells

For older children, you could stick small shells and starfish inside the box, using a strong, general-purpose adhesive. Choose shells that they have collected themselves from the beach. For smaller children and babies, it is advisable not to put anything inside the box.

A simple boat shape and a seagull are given the same papier-mâché treatment. They are painted using poster colours and stuck onto the outside of the aquarium for decoration. Once again, omit these shapes if you have very small children, as they will quickly pull them from the sides of the box.

1 *Remove the flaps from the top of the cardboard box to leave a clean, open edge to form the front of the aquarium. Use either the box flaps, or other offcuts of card, to make a wavy edging around the open end of the box. Cut the edging with sharp scissors in several separate pieces to make the task easier.*

5 *Cut the fishes from the bottles, having first removed the screw top necks. Cut the rigid base from each bottle, then squeeze the end together and cut out a tail. Secure the tail with staples or paper clips and cover the entire fish with two layers of tissue paper and paste. Leave to dry.*

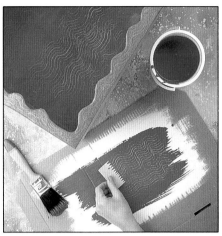

**2** Stick the waves onto the box using strips of newspaper and wallpaper paste. Wrap some around the edges of the waves and take others from the waves onto the box for strength. Cover the box, inside and out, at the same time, allowing each layer to dry before adding another. Apply three layers in all.

**3** Paint the interior and exterior of the box with white emulsion and leave to dry. Then apply a layer of bright blue emulsion and, while the paint is still wet, draw wiggly lines through it to simulate waves. Make these lines using a comb cut from a piece of thin card. Practise the technique first on an offcut.

**4** Tint ordinary white emulsion with a little blue poster paint until you reach a good pale blue, then thin this with an equal quantity of tap water to make a runny paint. Use this to create splatters that will simulate the foaming surf. Strike one decorator's brush against another to make the splatters.

**6** When the fish are dry, remove the staples or paper clips and cover the holes with more tissue paper. Paint in eye details using black poster colour. Make a small slit in the top of each fish, large enough to pass a knotted length of string or fishing line through, then seal the slit with more paste and tissue.

**7** Thread the other end of the string through a long needle and push this through the roof of the aquarium. Tie the string into a large knot to secure the fish once it is at the required level. Children will inevitably try to pull the fish out, so the larger the knot, the more difficult this will be.

**8** Cut the seagull and the boat from pieces of thin card, using the patterns provided. Cover with a layer of newspaper and paste, and allow to dry. Paint with white emulsion, then colour with bright poster paints. Glue the boat onto the side of the aquarium, and the seagull onto the top.

**Left and below:** *If you wish, you can decorate the aquarium with these seagull and sailboat shapes. Use the patterns full size, tracing them from the page and copying them onto card. Cut the shapes out, cover them with a layer of papier-mâché and paint with white emulsion and then poster colours. Finally, glue them on the aquarium.*

# CAT MIRROR

*This colourful cat can be suspended from the ceiling or hung on a wall, whichever you prefer. Either way, it will delight and amuse small children as they stretch up to see their faces in the mirror.*

If you want to hang this delightful mirror from the ceiling, it is best placed in the corner of a room or in an alcove. This means that a child will be able to touch and play with the cat, and it will wobble and bob about on its string, but it will not spin round and round in circles, making it safer for a smaller child.

## Enlist Some Help
A fret saw is easy to use with a little practice, especially if you enlist the help of a friend to hold the hardboard flat on the edge of a worktop as you saw. They will also be able to turn the board as you progress, making this whole process a lot easier. As you cut around the shape, the saw will only be able to progress by an amount equal to the depth of its frame, so you will need to cut off portions of the hardboard in order to continue.

**You will need:**
Hardboard
Chalk and ruler
Fret saw
White emulsion paint
Decorator's brush
Poster colours
Artist's brush
Mirror
String or ribbon
Bradawl
General-purpose glue

Once the shape of the cat has been cut out, it only requires a coat of white emulsion before you can begin enjoying the process of painting it. If you are uncertain of your artistic skills and do not think that you could do a good job, the cat could be finished with a uniform colour, such as black or orange, or even a fantasy colour such as blue or pink. However, it is worth trying your hand at creating this attractive ginger striped cat, as any child would adore it.

## Finding a Mirror
The mirror is simply fixed onto the surface of the hardboard cat using a strong, general-purpose adhesive. If you have trouble in finding a suitable round mirror for the cat, you could buy an inexpensive two-sided vanity mirror instead. By splitting open its frame, you will be able to release and use one of the two separate mirrors inside.

## Pierce a Hole
You need to make a small hole in the centre of the cat's back through which to thread the hanging string or ribbon. You will find the optimum place for the hole by holding the cat along this edge with your thumb and forefinger, and slowly moving your grip along its back until a balance is found. Pierce the hole by working a bradawl through the hardboard at this point.

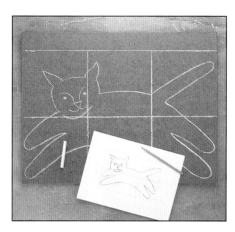

**1** *Copy the shape of the cat onto the hardboard, using the simple grid technique to enlarge it to the appropriate size. We used white chalk to draw the outline, as this is clearly visible when you are cutting the shape out. However, you could use a marker pen instead.*

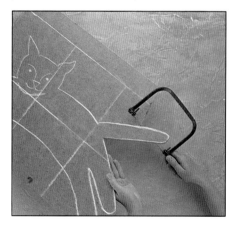

**2** *Use the fret saw to cut carefully around the outline, using the method outlined in the Introduction. You will need to remove sections of the hardboard as you progress, since the saw will only cut to the depth allowed by its frame.*

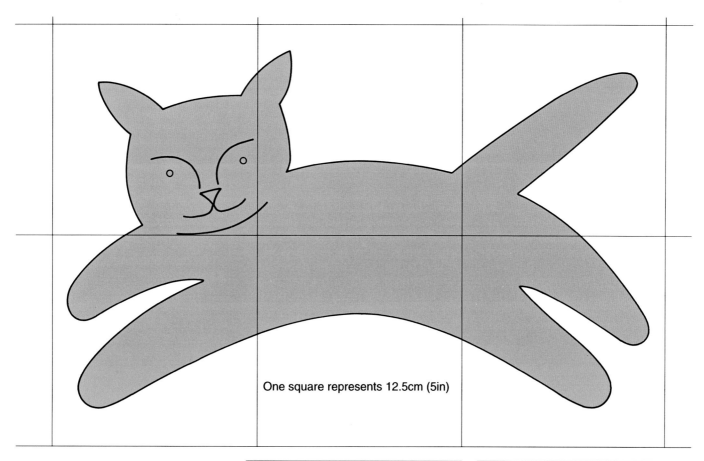

One square represents 12.5cm (5in)

**Above:** *To make the cat's body, scale-up this pattern using the simple grid technique explained in the Introduction. You can do this directly onto the sheet of hardboard, using chalk or a marker pen. Then cut out the cat with a fret saw.*

**Left:** *This charming cat mirror will provide hours of enjoyment as your child stretches to see into the looking glass. Hang it on a wall or from the ceiling where it will wobble and bob about on its ribbon as your child reaches for it.*

**3** *Paint the cat with a layer of white emulsion paint and allow it to dry. Dash in broad squiggles of brown, orange, yellow and black poster colours to form the markings, and paint in the face details.*

**4** *Soften the rough squiggles with a clean, damp paint brush, blurring the edges together. Add the paw details and leave to dry. Glue the mirror in the centre of the body, then punch a hole along the back and thread with ribbon.*

# THE COW JUMPED OVER THE MOON LIGHTSHADE

*This lightshade was inspired by a nursery rhyme. Although it doesn't actually shade the bulb, the latter looks like a star nestling close to the moon. The moon itself is constructed from layers of yellow tissue paper over a wire frame, while a painted cardboard cow is suspended over it.*

**You will need:**
Medium-gauge and florist's wire
Wire cutters and pliers
Scissors
Pencil and ruler
Yellow tissue paper
Wallpaper paste
Stiff card
Newspaper
White emulsion paint
Brush
Black and pink poster paints
Fishing line

The hollow nature of this golden moon makes it glow when the bulb is alight. It is constructed from two separate crescents of medium-gauge wire, available from most hardware stores. The two crescents are bound together using lengths of florist's wire to create a three-dimensional structure. Pieces of coloured tissue paper are glued around the moon, and as they dry out, the lightshade becomes quite rigid. It is important to lay large pieces of tissue paper over the frame rather than small pieces, because the whole structure is rather fragile until it is covered. A small piece of wire is allowed to project beyond the tissue paper, and is bent into a hook with a pair of pliers, allowing the moon to be fixed to the electrical flex.

You will need to change an ordinary light bulb for a low-wattage, golf ball bulb to reduce the amount of heat emitted. The tiny round bulb will also look like a star close to the

**Right:** *Just like the nursery rhyme character, this cardboard cow appears to jump over the moon whenever the light is switched on.*

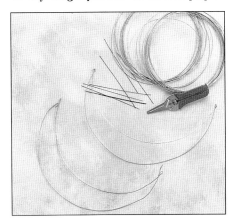

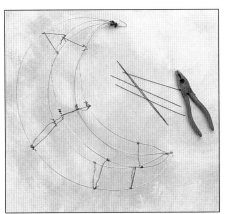

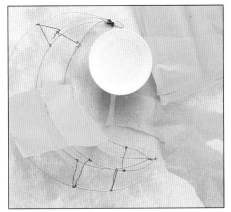

**1** *Cut two lengths of wire, about 84cm (33in) long, adding an extra 5cm (2in) to one length to form the hook. Bend the ends of the wires into tiny hooks and lock them together with pliers. Repeat with the other ends, leaving the longer one protruding. Bend the wires to form a crescent. Repeat with two more wires of equal length.*

**2** *Cut a fifth length of wire and shape into a curve, place between the wire crescents and join it to their ends. Use lengths of the florist's wire to bind the crescents together to form the three-dimensional moon shape. Make sure the structure is strong enough to maintain its shape while you cover it with paper. Bend the protruding wire into a hook.*

**3** *Tear large strips of yellow tissue paper from a sheet and brush paste over the torn edges. Lay the strips over the wire frame, maintaining a single layer of paper over the whole surface of the moon so that light can pass through it. Overlap the strips of paper at the edges and stick down with paste. Trim off any excess paper with scissors.*

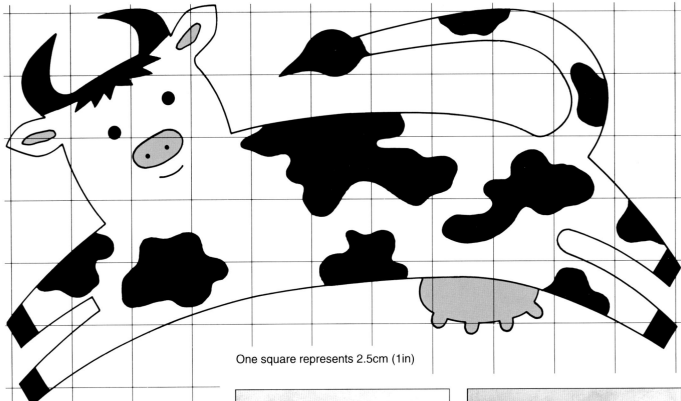

One square represents 2.5cm (1in)

**Above:** *Use the grid technique described in the Introduction to enlarge this pattern for the cow. Then cut the cow from stiff or corrugated cardboard.*

moon. It is vital not to allow the bulb to touch the shade; this could be dangerous.

The cow is constructed from a piece of stiff or corrugated card, and painted on both sides with poster colours. It is hung from the top point of the moon using fishing line. Once again, ensure that the line does not hang too close to the light bulb or touch it at any point.

We painted the plastic bulb holder with a matching yellow paint. This needs to be a spray paint formulated for use on plastics.

**4** *Cut the cow from stiff card and cover with a layer of papier-mâché, using small strips of newspaper and wallpaper paste. Allow to dry, then paint with enough white emulsion to cover the paper evenly. When this has dried, add the cow's markings and facial features with black and pink poster paints.*

**5** *Make a small hole in the cow's back, thread fishing line through it and knot. Tie the other end to the hook at the top of the moon, adjusting the line until the cow looks as if it is jumping over the moon. Hook the moon over the flex, making sure that neither the moon nor the fishing line touches the bulb.*

# BUNNY BLANKET MOTIF

*Suitable for the tiniest of newborn babies, a toddler or a young child, this motif makes an eye-catching decoration for any plain blanket for the cot, pram or bed. The handsome rabbit is made using a simple appliqué technique, with a pretty gingham fabric for its waistcoat.*

**You will need:**
Pencil and rule
Pins
Brown paper
Iron
Double-sided iron-on interfacing
White cotton fabric
Gingham
Thread
Scissors

You really need a sewing machine for this design, as it would take a long time to stitch purely by hand. Coloured thread is used to outline the white rabbit so that it will show up even when attached to a white blanket. Iron-on fabric interfacing, pressed onto the reverse side of the fabric that forms the rabbit's body, bonds the rabbit to the blanket.

Transfer the rabbit design onto the white cotton, using the grid technique. Cut the rabbit's waistcoat from a piece of blue gingham fabric, and pin this carefully onto the rabbit. You could use any patterned fabric you like for the waistcoat, changing the colour of the thread around the rabbit accordingly.

## Zig-zag Stitch

Set your sewing machine to a close zig-zag stitch and sew all around the outline of the rabbit, and around the edges of the waistcoat as you go. A stitching line is also sewn down the middle of the rabbit's waistcoat. The rabbit's facial features can be sewn by machine or by hand, using the illustration outlined on page 71. The excess cotton fabric is then trimmed away from around the rabbit shape.

After removing the backing paper from the interfacing fabric, simply press the motif into position with an iron. The hot iron bonds the motif effortlessly onto the blanket.

**1** *Transfer the rabbit shape onto brown paper and cut out the pattern. Iron the interfacing onto the reverse of the white cotton fabric, then draw around the pattern on the front of the cotton using a pencil. Cut a waistcoat for the rabbit from patterned fabric.*

**2** *Pin the waistcoat onto the body of the rabbit, aligning the armholes and the curve of the neck. Set the sewing machine to a close zig-zag stitch and follow the outlines carefully, turning the fabric as it moves under the sewing foot. Then stitch the rabbit features.*

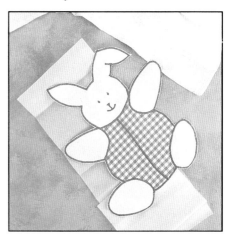

**3** *Cut away the excess cotton fabric and interfacing, leaving the stitching around the edge of the rabbit intact. Remove the backing paper from the interfacing and position the motif on the blanket. Use a hot iron to bond the motif to the blanket.*

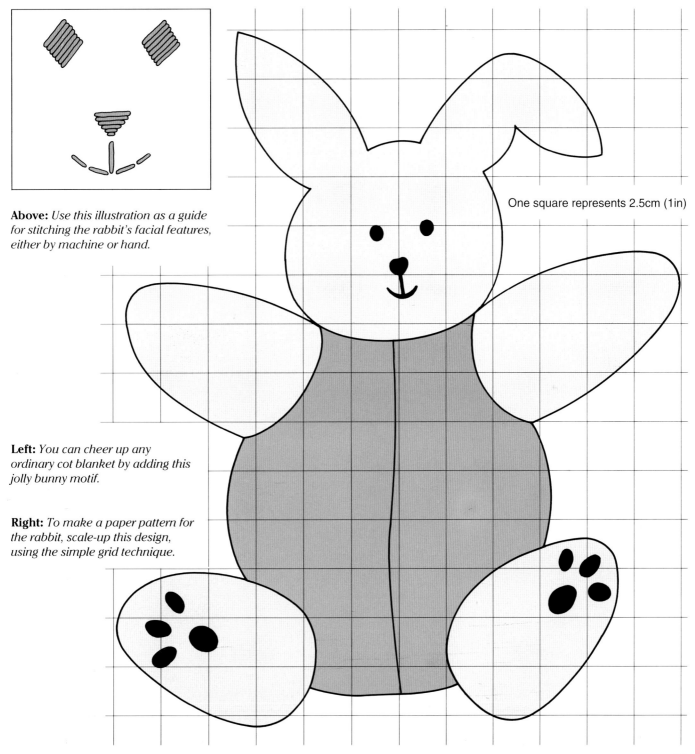

One square represents 2.5cm (1in)

**Above:** *Use this illustration as a guide for stitching the rabbit's facial features, either by machine or hand.*

**Left:** *You can cheer up any ordinary cot blanket by adding this jolly bunny motif.*

**Right:** *To make a paper pattern for the rabbit, scale-up this design, using the simple grid technique.*

# BABY TOWEL

*This soft, fluffy towel is edged with a pretty border of yellow gingham. The triangular hood slips over the head, while the generous folds of the towel swaddle the baby, snug and warm after a bath.*

Baby towels rarely come in any colour other than pure white, so this delightful towel would make a very special gift or colourful addition to the nursery.

Towelling can be purchased by the metre or yard at most fabric stores, and it comes in a wide range of colours. The hood is simply a square of towelling folded in half, edged with a little gingham across the folded edge, and inset into one of the corners. A gingham binding is then stitched around the raw edges to finish the towel neatly.

Edge the towel with the fabric of your choice. We decided upon a co-ordinating fabric, but you may prefer to edge your towel using a strong, contrasting or a patterned fabric. When choosing the fabric, check the washing instructions to ensure that the colours will not run so that the towel can be washed easily in a washing machine - non-fast colours will run in the wash and spoil the towelling. The strips can be machine stitched onto the towel, but the overlapping corners must be sewn under by hand.

**Right:** *This soft, hooded towel, with its pretty gingham border, will keep your baby snug and warm after a bath. It is easy to make and will prove a useful addition to any nursery.*

 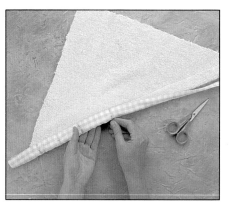 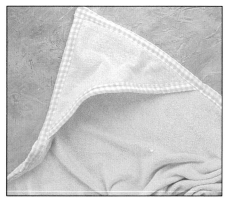

**1** *Cut the basic towel shape from a single thickness of towelling, 90x100cm (36x40in), cutting out a separate square for the hood, 28x28cm (11x11in). Shake the towelling pieces to remove the loose bits of cotton from the cut edges. Fold the hood square in half across the diagonal to form a triangle of a double thickness of towelling.*

**2** *Cut five 10cm (4in) wide strips of gingham to edge the towel and the hood. Sew the edging strip face down onto one side of the hood, 4cm (1½in) from the fold, leaving a 1cm (½in) seam allowance, with the raw edge facing the fold. Turn the strip back over the fold to the other side, turn under the raw edge and pin, then stitch, in place.*

**3** *Pin the hood onto one corner of the towel. Lay a strip of binding, wrong side up, on the back of the towel, stitch it about 4cm (1½in) from the edge, leaving a 1cm (½in) seam allowance. Fold the strip over to the other side of the towel, trapping the raw edges, and turn under a 1cm (½in) seam. Pin, then stitch, repeating on all sides.*

# RAGGEDY RABBITS

*These charming toys look as if they have been passed down through the generations, but in fact, it is tea that gives these rabbits their characteristic faded look. They have been sewn from offcuts of cotton and soaked overnight in a bowl of tea.*

Choose an open-weave cotton fabric to make these rabbits: a cheese-cloth or thick muslin is ideal. The heads and bodies of the rabbits are made from one piece of fabric, the legs, ears and arms being sewn onto this. The pieces are stuffed with a soft filling; look for a toy stuffing that has been tested to rigorous safety standards.

Once the toy has been stuffed and sewn together, make up a bowl of tea, using two tea bags to around 850ml (1½pints) of boiling water. Allow the tea to infuse and, when it has cooled to body temperature, push the toy under, until the filling has taken up the tea, and leave to soak overnight; then wring it out and hang it from its ears on a washing line to dry. Keep it away from other washing in case the tea drips onto it.

Once the rabbit is dry, it can be dressed in simple clothing, such as the dress or gingham shorts shown here. The features are stitched onto its face in black embroidery thread, using two French knots for the eyes and straight stitches forming its nose and mouth.

**Right:** *The secret of these lovable faded rabbits that look like heirlooms is tea. Once sewn together, the soft toys are soaked in a bowl of tea, which gives them their aged appearance.*

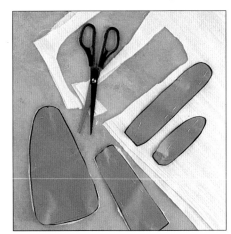

**1** *Scale-up the body shapes to make paper patterns, using the grid technique. Lay the patterns onto a double thickness of the cotton fabric and pin around the edges. Cut around each shape carefully, using sharp scissors.*

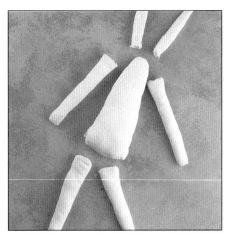

**2** *Stitch the pairs of shapes together, close to the edges, leaving a small gap in each seam. Turn the shapes right sides out, then stuff each piece with the toy filling and hand stitch the gap closed. Carefully stitch the limbs onto the body.*

**3** *Make up a bowl of tea and allow to infuse. When the tea has cooled, push the rabbit into the solution. Press it down until it is completely submerged and leave overnight. Squeeze over a sink and hang up to dry.*

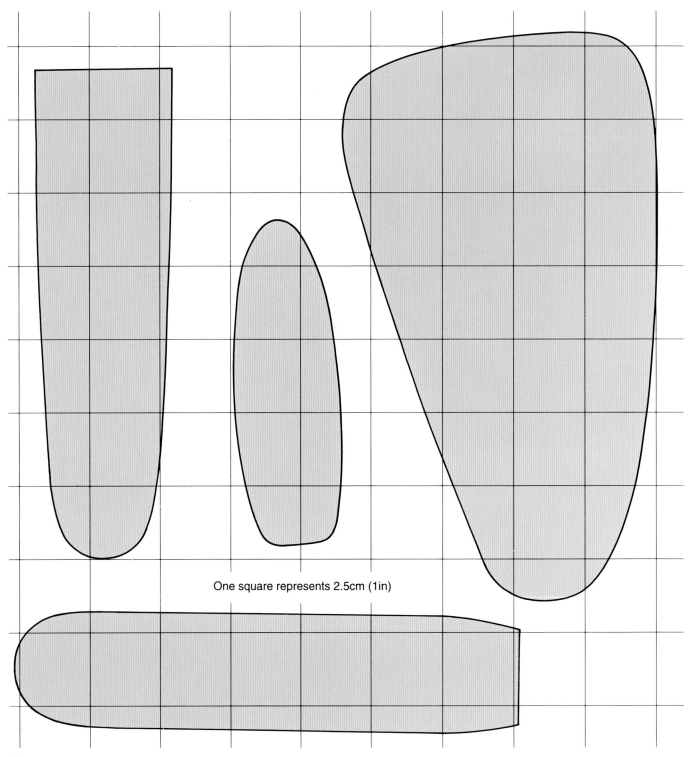

One square represents 2.5cm (1in)

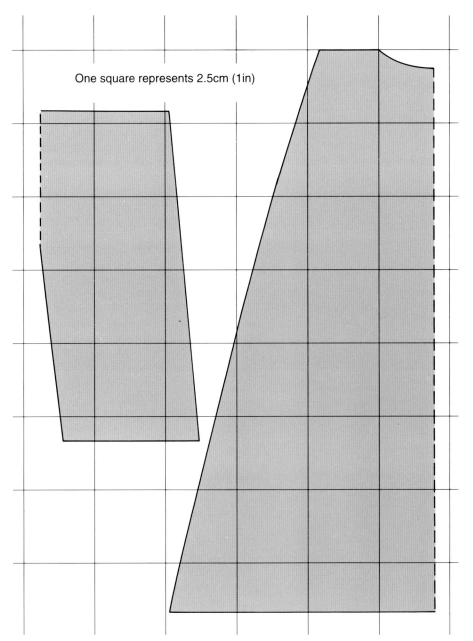

One square represents 2.5cm (1in)

4 *To make a female rabbit, cut out two dress halves, scaling-up the pattern provided. Sew them together, face to face, down the sides and across the shoulders, and turn right sides out. Turn under the raw edges on the neck, arm holes and hem. Slip onto the rabbit and tie on a ribbon waistband.*

5 *To make a male rabbit, scale-up the pattern for the shorts, using the grid technique, and cut from a double thickness of your fabric. Sew small pieces of ribbon across the bottoms of the shorts and across the waistband. Then stitch the front and back together and slip onto the rabbit.*

**Left:** *To make the basic rabbit, scale-up the patterns provided using the grid technique explained in the Introduction. The patterns are, clockwise from top left, leg, ear, body and arm shapes. Make brown paper patterns and use to cut the pieces from a double layer of fabric.*

**Above:** *Scale-up these patterns to make shorts or a simple shift dress, depending on whether the rabbit is to be male or female. Cut from two layers of fabric, placed back to back, and folded in half. The dotted line on the pattern should lay along the fold of the fabric.*

# DOLL'S HOUSE CUPBOARD

*This delightful cupboard was originally picked up in a junk shop, but with a little paint, it has been transformed into a wonderful piece of furniture that can be used for storing toys or clothes in the nursery.*

When you are looking for a suitable cupboard to paint, scour junk shops and car boot sales for something old, or look for a new cupboard of the right proportions in a furniture or DIY shop. You will need to strip the old finish from a secondhand cupboard, using paint stripper. Work outside, or in a well-ventilated room, as the fumes can be noxious; always wear rubber gloves.

If you are able to buy a new piece of untreated furniture, with no wax or polish on it at all, you can paint it straight away with no preparation being needed. Sometimes a furniture dealer may let you have the piece for a little less than the retail price if you are buying it in its raw state. However, if your cupboard is new and has a waxed surface, you will need to rub this down, using a pad of wire wool soaked in white spirit. Wipe the surface with warm soapy water after this treatment.

## A Good Surface
Once the furniture has been prepared, you can begin painting. First you will need to prepare a good surface for the paint. Apply one coat of white, acrylic wood primer/sealer and allow to dry. Then apply a coat of a coloured base paint; we used a mid-blue emulsion paint for this cupboard, but terracotta or cream would work just as well. Then we used a slightly thinned white emulsion paint to create the scumbled

**You will need:**
Cupboard
Primer/sealer
Decorator's brush
Emulsion paints
Wallpaper offcuts
Wallpaper paste and brush
Pencil
Rule and tape measure
Masking tape
Fine artist's brush
Varnish

**1** *Remove the door knobs before painting, unless they are wooden. Paint the cupboard with a coat of acrylic primer and allow to dry, then apply the base colour. Mix equal quantities of white emulsion paint with water and use a scrubbing motion with the brush to apply a scumbled finish to the base coat.*

surface. The paint is applied using a scrubbing action with the brush, rubbing the colour onto the cupboard in all directions until it develops this attractive broken surface.

## Add the Doors and Windows
When the surface of the paint is completely dry, use a pencil and rule to draw the door and window details. The size of these details will depend on the proportions of your cupboard. We painted a tall, thin cupboard, which lends itself to a three-storey house, but your cupboard may be smaller and wider, in which case the windows and door must be scaled to match these proportions. If you are unsure about how the windows should look, cut a range of different window shapes from paper and use temporary sticky pads to move them around on the cupboard until you are satisfied.

Unless the cupboard is very large, arrange the windows in a line down the centre of each cupboard door, using a tape measure to find the centreline. Divide each window into square glazing panels and add a window sill. Draw the doorway in the same way, and follow our step-by-step instructions for painting.

The cupboard should be sealed with varnish to protect the painted surface. We used an acrylic, water-based varnish, which is convenient, as the brushes can be washed out in water. It also has a shorter drying time than polyurethane varnish.

**Right:** *This imaginative treatment will turn an old or unexciting cupboard into a wonderful nursery accessory.*

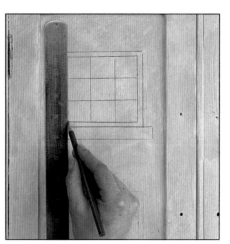

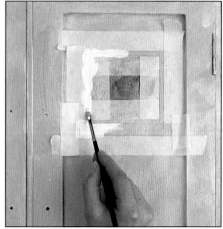

**2** Line the inside of the cupboard with an assortment of patterned wallpapers. Measure each shelf and shelf back, and cut a piece of paper to fit exactly. Use wallpaper paste to stick the paper in place. The different papers can suggest different rooms if the cupboard is used as a doll's house.

**3** Decide on the size and positioning of the windows and door, then use a pencil and rule to draw their outlines on the cupboard. Divide the windows into separate glazed panels, and add door panels for an attractive look. Finally, draw a sill under each window, and steps leading up to the door.

**4** Use masking tape to create a sharp edge for the painted windows and doorway, aligning it with the pencil lines. First mask over the window frame and paint in the area of 'glass', using a thin grey emulsion. Mask off this area when dry, place tape around the outside of the window and paint the frame white.

**5** Next mask over the grey areas that you want to keep as 'glass', leaving 4mm (¼in) wide glazing bars. Press the sticky side of the masking tape against your clothing before use to remove some of its stickiness and protect the paint a little. Paint the glazing bars using the white emulsion and leave to dry.

**6** Use strips of masking tape to create a window sill and paint this area with white emulsion. We also added a white, brick-effect border down each side of the house. Remove the tape carefully so as not to remove the paint, but if the occasional chip does come off, touch-in the paint with a fine brush.

**7** Mask off the doorway in the same manner, and paint the whole door and step area white. Use grey emulsion to paint in the door panel and step edges, and a little yellow paint to simulate the door knob. Apply two coats of acrylic varnish to protect the finish. When dry, replace the door knobs.

# FABRIC-COVERED TOY BOX

*Transform an old chest into a bright, fabric-covered toy box, so that a small child will be just as amused by the characters decorating the outside of the box as by those to be found inside.*

This box was rescued from a jumble sale, obviously disregarded because of its shabby appearance. However, a little fabric, some wadding, a piece of self-adhesive felt and a staple gun soon changed this drab chest into a beautiful, softly-padded toy box.

First you need to cover the box with a soft wadding, and we chose wadding that is used for making quilts and has undergone important safety checks. This is vital for any materials used in the nursery.

Each side of the box is covered with a separate piece of fabric. This is stapled in place, keeping the line of staples hidden along the inside or under the base of the box, so that they cannot be seen from the outside. The staples on the inside can be disguised with a ribbon.

Self-adhesive felt is used to cover the inside of the lid. This gives a neat appearance to the box when the lid is lifted, and is also used to hide all the staples.

**You will need:**
Wooden chest
Fabric
Wadding
Staple gun
Scissors
Tape measure
Self-adhesive felt
Ribbon
Fabric glue

**Overleaf:** *This brightly-patterned, fabric-covered box can be used to store a multitude of books, games and toys, but it could also be used to contain bedlinen for the cot or bed. You can make it from any reclaimed chest, or a new one if you prefer.*

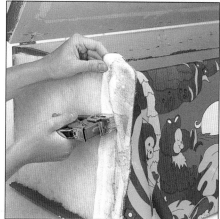

**1** *Cut five rectangles of wadding to fit the four sides of the box and the lid. Use a staple gun to secure the wadding to the box, preventing it from moving while you add the fabric. Use as few staples as possible, as the fabric will hold the wadding securely when it is stapled over it, and the staples will cause dimples on the surface.*

**2** *Cut a piece of fabric to cover the front of the box, adding a 7.5cm (3in) seam allowance all round. Hold the fabric in place, turn the top edge inside and the bottom edge under the box, and staple in place. Work outwards from the centre, along the inside edge and base of the box. Repeat with the sides, stapling them to the box.*

**3** *Cut fabric to cover the sides of the box, adding the seam allowance as before. Hold the bulk of the fabric towards the front of the box, with the reverse side facing out, and staple a neat line down the side of the box towards the front. Fold the fabric back over these staples, concealing them and the staples holding the front piece of fabric in place.*

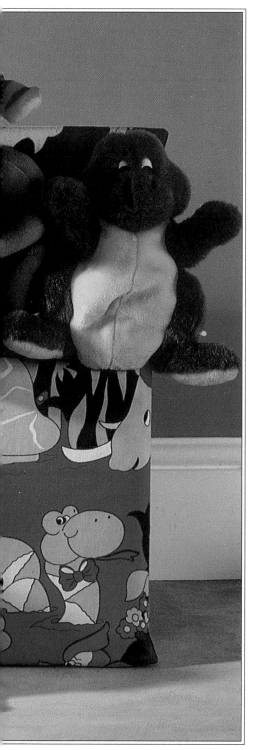

**4** *Smooth this piece of fabric over the side of the box, and fold over the top and bottom edges, as before. Staple in place, keeping the lines of staples along the inside of the box and underneath it. Keep the fabric taut to prevent it from sagging. Cover the remaining side of the box in the same manner.*

**5** *Place a piece of fabric on the lid of the box. Turn the excess to the underside of the lid and staple in place. Work from the centres of the longer sides first, moving outwards and keeping the fabric taut as you progress. Staple the shorter sides next, folding the corners into neat mitres before stapling in place.*

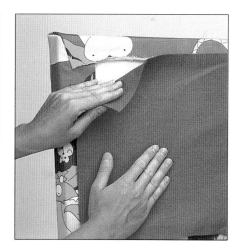

**6** *Cover the back of the box as the sides, holding the bulk of the fabric over one side of the box with the reverse facing out. Staple a neat line down the side. Then fold the fabric over this line, and progress as before, cutting around the hinges. The final line of staples will be unavoidably visible at the back.*

**7** *Cut a piece of self-adhesive felt to the size of the box lid, less 2.5cm (1in) all round, and use it to conceal all the staples. Stick one corner of the felt onto the box, then slowly peel away the backing paper, smoothing the felt onto the lid. Lastly, glue a ribbon around the rim of the box to cover the staples inside.*

# JUMPING JACK

*The Jumping Jack is a very old, traditional toy, which was not only used to entertain children, but also adults, in eighteenth-century France. Famous artists designed these fascinating toys, which come to life when the dangling string is tugged.*

This Jumping Jack is based on an old design of the well-known Harlequin character, whose colourful clothing and masked face are traditional and distinctive features. The body parts are cut from hardboard, using a fret or power saw. Once all the pieces are cut, smooth the edges with fine-grade glass-paper.

Paint the pieces, front and back, with white emulsion paint, making sure you paint the narrow edges. Use our templates to trace off the details of the costume and the face mask, transferring the design to the front of the figure. This can then be painted, using bright poster colours. A yellow and red costume is traditional, but you could paint it in other colours if you prefer. It is only necessary to paint the front, as the other side will face the wall.

## Stringing the Figure

Once the parts are painted, the Harlequin is ready to be strung. A hole is made at the joint of each body section, at the point where the limb pivots. The thigh piece has a joint at both ends: one at the knee where the lower leg is connected, and one at the hip where it is fixed to the torso. We used a bradawl to make the holes.

Before the pieces are strung together, an extra hole is made below the first hole in each of the four limb pieces connected to the body (the arms and the thighs). These are used to move the limbs with the pulling string.

The joints are all connected with pieces of string, with the limbs being joined behind the torso. The string is knotted, then threaded through the hole in the body from the front, and through the hole in the limb behind it. The string is then knotted again, as tightly as possible behind the limb, and the excess cut off. Repeat this until all the pieces are joined to form the complete Harlequin.

## Connect the Pulling String

Use the second set of holes to string the figure so that it moves when the pulling string is tugged. Lay the figure down so that the arms are hanging straight behind the body. Thread thin string through the hole in one arm and knot at the front. Bring the string across at the back and thread through the hole in the other arm. Tie the string at the front of the other arm so it is taut when the arms are hanging down. Connect the legs in the same way. Then join the centres of these strings with another piece, allowing the end to hang between the legs to form the pulling string.

Tie a bead onto the end of the pulling string and attach a string to the head, from which to hang the figure. The limbs of the Jumping Jack will jerk up and down as the pulling string is tugged.

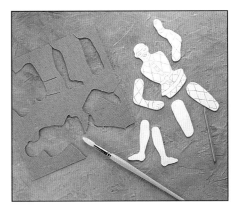

**1** *Cut all the Harlequin body parts from a piece of hardboard, using the templates provided, and smooth the edges with glass-paper. Paint both surfaces with white emulsion, remembering to paint the narrow edges of the pieces.*

**Right:** *This traditional Jumping Jack will provide constant entertainment for your child, its arms and legs moving up and down in unison as the pulling string is tugged. The colourful design is based on the Harlequin.*

**2** *Trace off the details of the Harlequin costume from the patterns and transfer the details onto the figure's body and limbs. Colour the costume with bright poster paints, either the red and yellow shown or some other contrasting hues. Use black to pick out the details. Punch holes in the limbs with a bradawl for the string joints.*

**3** *Tie all the limb pieces together, then string up the Harlequin carefully, using the method described in the text and referring to the diagram above right. If the pulling string does not work effectively at your first attempt, go through the procedure again until it does. Attach a string to the head from which to hang the toy on the wall.*

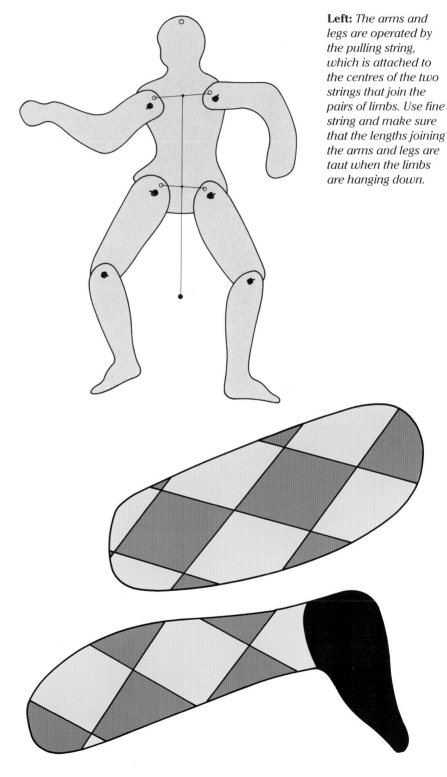

**Left:** *The arms and legs are operated by the pulling string, which is attached to the centres of the two strings that join the pairs of limbs. Use fine string and make sure that the lengths joining the arms and legs are taut when the limbs are hanging down.*

**Right and below left:** *To make the various pieces of the Jumping Jack, use these full-size patterns, tracing them from the page and transferring them to a piece of hardboard. After cutting them out with a fret saw, the pieces can be coloured with poster paints to the design shown in colours of your choice. After stringing the pieces together and checking that the Jumping Jack works as it should, hang the figure from the wall where it can be reached by your child.*

# COT STORAGE POUCH

*This pretty pouch is designed to be attached to the side of a cot, using fabric ties that are fastened around the bars in a bow. When the baby is young and the base of the cot is at its highest setting, the pouch pockets inside the cot are tucked under the mattress, but as the baby grows and the mattress is moved down, the pockets inside become useful for storing books and toys.*

This pouch is made from a double thickness of fabric, edged with a simple border. Large pockets are sewn onto the fabric, with stitching from top to bottom forming three separate pockets. We selected a border fabric that co-ordinated well with the colours of the base fabric. Choose a soft, subtle pattern so that the pocket fabric stands out.

The outside pockets can be used for nappies, packets of baby wipes, paper tissues, cotton wool, and so on. The inside pockets are used for books and toys to amuse the child.

## Fabric Requirements
Make sure that all the fabrics are compatible for washing with colours that will not run. Cut all the pieces before you begin. You will need a double thickness rectangle of base fabric, 100x80cm (40x32in), plus a few offcuts for the ties; we used a soft green check. For the border, we used matching green stripes; you will need two strips 10x100cm (4x40in) and two 10x80cm (4x32in). You will also need two rectangles, 66x56cm (26x22in), of a patterned fabric to form the pockets.

## You will need:

Base fabric: 2 pieces 100x80cm
(40x32in) and offcuts to make ties
Border fabric: 2 pieces 100x10cm
(40x4in) and 2 pieces 80x10cm
(32x4in)
Pocket fabric: 2 pieces 66x56cm
(26x22in)
Dressmaker's pins
Thread
Scissors
Needle
Sewing machine (optional)
Tape measure
Pencil

**Left:** *This simple storage pouch drapes over the side of a cot, and is as useful as it is colourful. You can fill the outer pockets with a variety of essential nursery items, such as nappies, wipes and cotton wool. The inner pockets can hold toys or books that will keep your child amused.*

**1** *Turn a 1cm (½in) seam allowance under along the long sides of the border strip and fold in half. Pin, then stitch two shorter strips onto the sides of the main fabric. Make a dart at both ends of the longer strips and sew in place; the darts produce neat mitres at the ends of the fabric.*

**2** *Cut two rectangles from a patterned fabric to form the pockets. Turn under a small hem along all the sides, then fold the rectangles in half to make the pieces 33x56cm (13x22in). Pin, then stitch around the three open sides of both pockets, as close to the edge as possible, forming a double-thickness rectangle.*

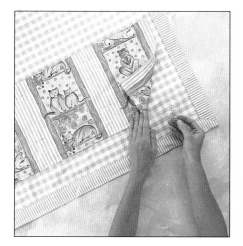

**3** *Pin the pockets onto the base fabric. They should be arranged centrally along the width of the fabric, with the bottom edges 12.5cm (5in) away from the border at each end. Stitch each pocket to the fabric around three sides, with the openings facing each other towards the centre of the base fabric.*

**4** *Sew two vertical lines of stitching through all thicknesses of fabric, from the top to the bottom of each large pocket, to create three smaller pockets. Extend the stitching line backwards and forwards a few times at the top and bottom of each line to strengthen the seam and prevent it coming unstitched.*

**5** *Make the ties, using eight strips of fabric, 11.5x28cm (4½x11in). Fold each strip in half along its length, with right sides facing. Sew down the long, open edge and across one of the ends. Turn the tie right sides out, using a pencil if necessary, and sew the open end onto the pouch, tucking the raw ends inside.*

# Sailboat Blind

*These attractive sailboats have actually been made from small pieces of driftwood, collected from the beach, stuck together and painted. The boats can be used to edge a blind or curtain, along with small shells and pebbles, cork beads and starfish for a distinctive seashore theme.*

You only need a few pieces of driftwood to make a convincing boat: a piece for the hull, another for the boathouse and a couple of smaller pieces for the funnels. Use a strong wood glue to stick them together, allowing it to set before painting the boats. Use poster colours to add the details; small, round portholes make the boats convincing.

Small silver jewellery rings are stuck to the top of the boathouse at a point where the boat is perfectly balanced. To find this spot, hold the boat lightly between thumb and forefinger along the top edge and see if it hangs straight or at an angle. If necessary, move your grip until perfect balance is achieved, then attach the ring at the same point.

Thread nylon fishing line through the ring and tie securely, snipping off the excess. A few small beads can be threaded onto the line to make the mobile boat more attractive. Use a needle to stitch the line securely onto the hem of the curtain or blind. Repeat this procedure with shells, starfish and pebbles. You will need to find pebbles with holes in them, but starfish can be threaded onto the line using a needle.

**Right:** *Give your nursery's blind or curtain a distinct feel of the seashore by turning it into a mobile with little driftwood boats, shells, starfish and pebbles collected from the beach. Suspend them from nylon fishing line decorated with coloured and cork beads for added interest.*

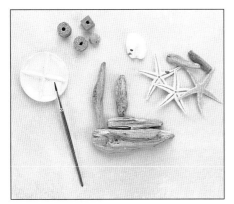

**1** *Assemble the small driftwood boats, using two long, flat pieces of wood for the hull and boathouse, and two smaller sticks for the funnels. Glue the pieces together, using a strong wood adhesive, and allow to dry before painting the boats.*

**2** *Once the glue has dried, use bright poster colours to paint the boats. Do not use too much paint, as the natural colours of the driftwood should still be visible. Having found the balance point, glue a small silver jewellery ring to the top of each boathouse.*

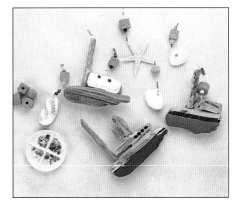

**3** *Tie a length of fishing line to the ring and thread coloured and cork beads onto it. Repeat these steps for other items such as starfish, shells and pebbles. Thread the line through the eye of a large needle and stitch each mobile onto the curtain or blind hem.*

# POT OF FLOWERS

*This brightly-painted pot of flowers brings a real splash of colour to a nursery. The pot is filled with plaster of Paris for stability, and is perfect for the top of a shelf unit, windowsill or chest of drawers.*

**You will need:**
Cardboard
Pencil and ruler
Paper
Scissors
Newspaper
Wallpaper paste and brush
White and blue emulsion
Wire and wire cutters
Poster colours and brush
Masking tape
Terracotta pot
Dry oasis foam
Plaster of Paris
Varnish
Craft knife
Yellow ricrac and glue

These quirky tulips and leaves are made from corrugated cardboard. We used three tulip heads and five leaves for the pot. The flower heads and leaves are covered with papier-mâché.

Lengths of medium-gauge wire are used as stalks; these are also covered with papier-mâché. Once the flowers are in place, they can be bent into any position you like.

Use layers of newspaper and wallpaper paste to make papier-mâché, allowing each layer to dry out before

**Left:** *For a splash of long-lasting colour, try these papier-mâché tulips in a brightly-painted flowerpot.*

applying the next. Drying can be accelerated by placing the leaves and flowers in an airing cupboard.

## Strong Tones

When three layers of paper have been applied, you can paint them. Apply white emulsion before adding any colour. Bright poster paints will create really strong tones. We used streaks of both light and dark green on the leaves, rather than painting in any one flat colour. Similarly, we streaked the tulip heads with red and orange or purple and pink paint.

Protect the papier-mâché leaves and flowers with two coats of acrylic varnish. Secure the flowers in oasis

in the bottom of the pot. Mix the plaster of Paris and pour the liquid into the pot, tapping it lightly to remove air bubbles. The plaster will quickly harden.

**1** *Copy and enlarge the flower and leaf shapes onto paper, using the grid as a guide. Use the resulting paper patterns to cut out as many flower heads and leaves as you need. You will find it easier to cut the card with a craft knife.*

**2** *Cut 30cm (12in) lengths of wire for the flower stalks and push the end of each inside the corrugations at the base of each flower. Repeat this for the leaves, using 15cm (6in) pieces of wire. Secure the wire with masking tape.*

**3** *Cover the flowers and leaves with strips of newspaper and wallpaper paste. Apply a layer of paper and leave to dry before applying the next layer. Wind newspaper strips around the wire stalks at the same time.*

One square represents 2.5cm (1in)

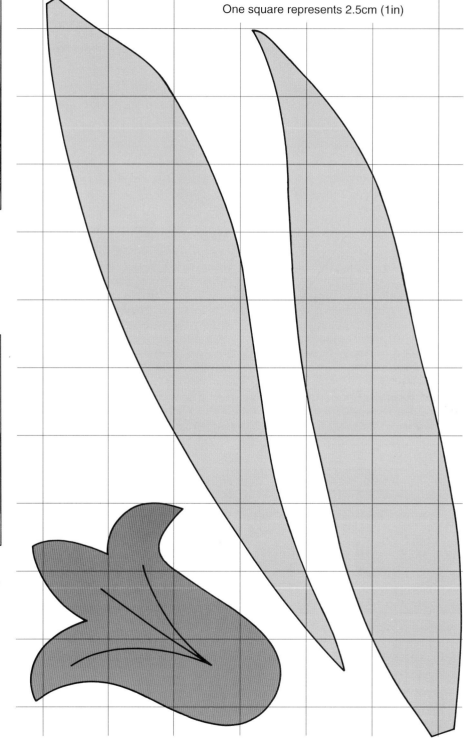

**4** *Paint the flowers and leaves, including the stalks, with a coat of white emulsion and allow to dry. Use poster colours to paint the bright flower heads and leaf stalks. Streak the paint to create interest on each leaf and flower.*

**5** *Varnish the leaves and flowers to protect, paint the flowerpot blue and stick on pieces of yellow ricrac. Push dry oasis foam into the bottom of the pot and insert the wire stalks. Mix up the plaster, pour on top and leave to harden.*

**Right:** *To make the flowers and leaves, scale-up these patterns, using the simple grid technique. Make paper templates and use them to cut the pieces from corrugated card.*

# INDEX

# ACKNOWLEDGEMENTS

*Nursery decorations and toys kindly supplied by:*

Descamps
Sloane Street
Chelsea
London
(0171) 236 6957

Anna French
343 King's Road
Chelsea
London
(0171) 737 6528

Peter Jones
Sloane Square
London SW3
(0171) 730 3434

The Kid's Company
81 Maple Road
Surbiton
Surrey
(0181) 390 5225

Meaker & Son
166 Wandsworth Bridge Road
London SW6
(0171) 731 7416

Paper Moon
53 Fairfax Road
London NW6
(0181) 451 2326

Squidgy Things
(0171) 833 5963


*Antique clothes from:*

Camden Passage
London
(Open Saturday and Wednesday)